走近长城

——遵化长城通览

Approaching the Great Wall

——A General Survey of Zunhua
Section of the Great Wall

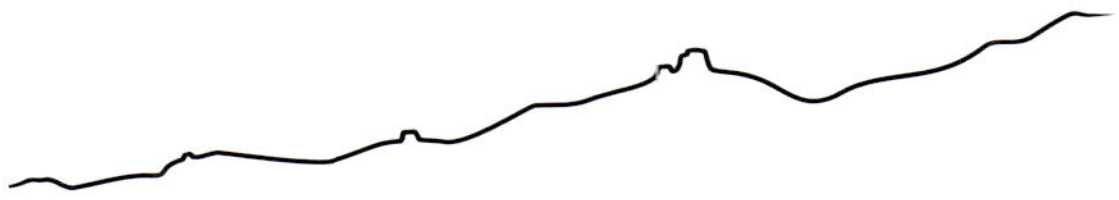

走近长城

韩保平 策划

Planned by Han Baoping

高景生 著

Written by Gao Jingsheng

遵化是中国长城荟萃之乡，
重叠环护的长城处处闪耀着中华民族智慧之光，
读懂了遵化长城也就读懂了中国长城。

Zunhua boasts an extraordinarily important section of the Great Wall in China,
Zunhua Section of the Great Wall sparkles with the extraordinary wisdom of the Chinese nation.
Comprehending Zunhua section of the Great Wall is to understand the Great Wall of China.

天胜寨长城

The Great Wall at Tiansheng Stockaded Village

走近长城

长城，之所以谓之为长城，一是修建时间长，上下两千年；二是总体跨度长，纵横十万里。春秋战国时，各诸侯国为抵御他国入侵，纷纷筑起由关隘、烽堠和城墙相连的防御工事，这就是中国最早的长城。秦始皇统一中国后，为防匈奴侵扰又将原秦、赵、燕长城连接增建，中国出现了东起辽东，西达临洮的第一道万里长城。继秦之后的汉、隋、唐、明等王朝为了中原安宁，不断在农耕与游牧交界地带增修加固长城，尤其是明朝，面对蒙古游牧部落日益频繁的侵袭，耗时200多年，构筑了从鸭绿江到嘉峪关跨越十省市自治区，长达8851.8公里具有综合防御作战能力的长城，创造了世界罕见的古建奇观。

奔腾于境北群山，集燕、北齐、明长城建筑艺术于一身，拱卫京师，呵护中原的遵化长城，是万里长城之精华。它东起遵迁交界的苇子岭，西达遵蓟搭边的凤凰岭，跨小厂、侯家寨、兴旺寨、西下营、汤泉、马兰峪、东陵七乡镇，全长138华里。洪山口、马蹄峪、罗文峪、沙坡峪、冷嘴头、大安口、鲇鱼石、马兰关、宽佃峪九座雄关横扼其间，是中原通往塞北的交通要道，是拒敌于关外的要冲隘口，更是农耕文化与游牧文化的交汇处，中原文明与草原文明的融合点。正所谓"万里长城谁为最，九关鱼钥控雄图。"纵观历史，遵化长城为中华民族的安宁、繁荣和昌盛做出过不可磨灭的贡献！

Approaching the Great Wall of China

The Great Wall is thus named for two reasons. Firstly, the construction time is long, spanning over two thousand years; and secondly, the overall structure is long, stretching for nearly fifty-thousand km. During the time of the Spring and Autumn period (770BC–476BC) and the subsequent Warring States period (475BC–221BC), the vassal states all constructed extensive fortifications, including passes, watchtowers, and walls to defend their own borders. These walls are the earliest part of the Great Wall in China. After unifying China, Qin Shi Huang, the first emperor of unified China, ordered the soldiers to join and expand the original walls built by Qin, Zhao and Yan states so as to guard against the attacks of the Huns. Therefore, there appeared China's first 5,000km-long wall extending from Liaodong in the east to Lintao in the west. After the Qin dynasty (221BC–206BC), the Han (206BC–220AD), Sui (581-618), Tang (618-907), and Ming (1368-1644) dynasties constantly rebuilt and enhanced the ancient wall at the borders between the farming and nomadic areas to safeguard the Central Plains. Especially the Ming dynasty, under the increasingly frequent invasions of nomadic Mongols, built an 8851.8km-long Great Wall, which was a comprehensive defense system that took 200 years to complete and stretched from the Yalu River to Jiayu Pass, covering ten provinces, and autonomous regions. That is an awe-inspiring wonder of the world of great antiquity.

Stretching across the steep mountains in northern China, Zunhua section of the Great Wall is the essential part of the entire megastructure, crystallizing the architectural essence of ancient Yan State, Northern Qi (550-577) and Ming dynasties, defending the capital city, and protecting the Central Plains. Measuring 138 *huali* (an ancient Chinese measurement unit; 1 *huali* is equivalent to about 415m) in length, this structure rises between Weizi Ridge in Zunhua City and Fenghuang Ridge in northeastern Hebei Province, covering seven towns and townships, namely, Xiaochang, Houjiazhai, Xingwangzhai, Xixiaying, Tangquan, Malanyu, and Dongling. Nine imposing passes, namely, Hongshan, Matiyu, Luowenyu, Shapoyu, Lengzuitou, Da'an, Nianyushi, Malan, and Kuandianyu, stand on traffic arteries that connect the Central Plains and the other side of the Great Wall. These passes are not only strategic military strongholds but also the combination of the farming culture of the Central Plains and nomadic culture of the grasslands. As the Chinese saying goes, "Which part of the Great Wall is the most prominent? The nine passes control the key to defend the territory." Throughout the Chinese history, Zunhua section of the Great Wall has made indelible contributions to the peace and prosperity of the Chinese nation!

作者简介

高景生，中国摄影家协会会员、中国长城学会会员、遵化市摄影家协会主席，平遥国际摄影艺术节"中国优秀画册"奖获得者（《走近清东陵》）、《人民日报》1994年度全国新闻摄影24强，曾为13位来遵化的党和国家领导人摄影，美国UPS全球快递公司中国大陆指定摄影师，2002年应邀以摄影师身份随中国对外友好协会代表团访美，在美国国会山为29位美国国会议员进行了肖像摄影，先后创作出版了《走近清东陵》、《走近遵化》、《光荣的遵化》、《绿色遵化》、《时代足迹 奋进遵化》等大型画册。他的清东陵和古长城系列摄影作品曾在中央电视台多套节目中播映。

About the Author

Gao Jingsheng is a member of the China Photographers' Society and the Great Wall Society of China, the President of Zunhua Photographers' Society, a winner of the Chinese Album of Excellence Award at the Pingyao International Photography Festival (*Approaching the Eastern Qing Tombs*), and one of the top 24 photojournalists in China rated by the *People's Daily* newspaper in 1994. He has taken photos of 13 party and state leaders visiting Zunhua. In 2002, he was invited to the United States as a photographer in a delegation of the Chinese People's Association for Friendship with Foreign Countries, and took photos of 29 congressmen of the United States at the Capitol Hill. He has published important albums such as *Approaching the Eastern Qing Tombs*, *Approaching Zunhua*, *Glorious Zunhua*, *Green Zunhua*, and *Footsteps of Times: Zunhua in Progress*. His series of photographic works on the Eastern Qing Tombs and the ancient Great Wall have been broadcast in several programs of China Central Television (CCTV).

走進長城 解讀長城

記録長城 保護長城

祝賀高景生先生《走近長城》攝影集出版發行　鈕祜祿茂生

钮祜禄茂生
原为水利部长、河北省省长、
中国长城学会常务副会长

Niohru Maosheng
Former Minister of Water Resources and Governor of Hebei Province
Vice President of the Great Wall Society of China

序 ——

中国的万里长城是人类文明史上一个令人骄傲的伟大存在。长城沿线有许多城市、乡镇、村落都保存着精彩的历史遗迹，它们共同构成伟大存在的点点滴滴，汇聚成为辉煌的整体。

现在大家看到的这本《走近长城》是讲述河北遵化从东到西、由古及今的长城故事，应该说就是万里长城伟大遗存的一个非常精彩的局部。按这本书介绍，在遵化有古老的燕长城和北齐长城，还有东西长达138华里的明长城。它号称有九门雄关，下设二十二寨，都有详尽的图片加以描述。又介绍说从洪武年间置卫，由徐达开始布关建寨，经过200多年不断施工，到崇祯年间完工，其间有戚继光筑城16年，为明长城的建成立下大功。遵化人非常珍惜古老长城记录下来的遥远而漫长的往事。明朝之后，有清一代及民国时期，直到我们生活着的现代中国的峥嵘岁月，遵化人都在传承长城开启的光荣遗存，又写下许多辉煌壮丽的崭新历史。

我很高兴遵化一位从事地方文化工作的高景生同志，因为担心长城历史与现实的传承和进步，用手中相机记录了关于文明成长的场景，编成一部内容丰富品味甚高的图册。唐山佰亿售电有限公司董事长韩保平慧眼识珠，支持图册出版，成就了弘扬长城文化的一桩盛事。对此，我和许多朋友一样感到振奋，这将是帮助我们的人民和青年了解长城这个伟大存在的好事，将推动我们生活中的文明进步，值得我们为之庆幸。

在遵化不仅有非常精彩的长城遗存，还有人民为创造新生活而拼搏奋斗的革命精神与历史上的人们修建长城的顽强实践有着真实的传承，这一点在这本图册中也有体现。高景生介绍了上个世纪五十年代的"穷棒子社"，毛主席曾誉之为"我们整个国家的形象"。六十年代沙石峪人民改天换地，周总理赞扬他们是"当代活愚公"。1966年我父亲陈毅元帅曾访问沙石峪，留诗一首。现在图册附上我父母双亲在沙石峪的留影。我想这是对五十年前一段历史的纪念，而这种纪念与长城所展示的中国文化千年进取的传统完全一致。我也题诗一首，表达感想并以此向读者朋友们致意。

长城内外是家乡，图册丰碑起颂扬。奋斗精神长屹立，世纪长城万里长。

陈昊苏

陈昊苏
原中国对外友好协会会长、
中国长城学会副会长

1966年4月29日，
陈毅夫妇随同周恩来总理访问沙石峪

Chen Yi and his wife visited
Shashiyu Village with Premier Zhou Enlai
on April 29, 1966.

Preface ——

The Great Wall of China is a pride of human civilization. Along the Great Wall, many cities, towns and villages have retained splendid historical monuments, which collectively form a cohesive and brilliant entirety.

This publication, *Approaching the Great Wall*, tells the story of the Zunhua section of the Great Wall in Hebei province, providing its details from the east to the west, and from the ancient times to present day. It can be regarded as a wonderful fragment of the great legacy of the Great Wall. According to this book, Zunhua boasts the ancient walls built by the Yan State and the Northern Qi Dynasty, and the 138 *huali*-long Great Wall of the Ming dynasty. It introduces readers to the nine passes and twenty-two stockaded villages with brief yet accurate descriptions. This book also mentions that garrisons were established during Emperor Hongwu's reign (1368-1398), and Xu Da initiated the construction of fortified villages. Through the following 200 years of continuous construction, the Great Wall was finally completed in the reign of Emperor Chongzhen (1628-1644). In particular, Qi Jiguang spent 16 years in directing the endeavor of city development, laying a remarkable foundation for the construction of the Great Wall. The people of Zunhua cherish the long history of Zunhua, which had left its mark on the ancient Great Wall. After the Ming dynasty, from the eventful years of the Qing dynasty (1644-1911), the Republic of China (1912-1949), to the modern China we live in today, Zunhua people not only carried forward the glorious legacy of the Great Wall, but also opened a splendid chapter in history.

I am glad to know that Mr. Gao Jingsheng, a local cultural worker of Zunhua who is concerned about the continuation and future of the Great Wall, records several sites related to the cultural development and compiles these photos into a high-quality and content-rich volume. Mr. Han Baoping, the president of Tangshan Baiyi Electronics Company, is a man of great insight and supports the publication of this book, which is a great contribution to promoting the Great Wall culture. In this regard, many friends and I are greatly inspired, because the publication will help our people and youth to better understand the significance of the Great Wall and promote the cultural development in our lives, which in turn will benefit us all.

In addition to wonderful relics of the Great Wall, Zunhua boasts the revolutionary spirit of hard-working people who strive to create a new life, and a solid legacy of unyielding practice in constructing the Great Wall historically, which is also presented in this book. Gao Jingsheng introduces the cooperative formed by poor peasants in the 1950s, which was recognized by Chairman Mao as the image of whole country. In the 1960s, the people of Shashiyu Village carried out a total renovation and transformation project, which was lauded by Premier Zhou Enlai as "the contemporary Foolish Old Man moving the mountain". In 1966, my father, Marshal Chen Yi, visited Shashiyu Village and composed a poem about this place. Now the photo of my parents is included in this book, which, in my opinion, is to commemorate a period of time fifty years ago. This historical memory is exactly in line with the centuries-old cultural tradition of diligence as displayed by the Great Wall. I also compose a poem to express my gratitude to the readers.

Homeland extends beyond the Great Wall; acclaim fills book pages. Long stands the spirit of resilience and perseverance, and long stands the monumental Great Wall.

Chen Haosu

Former President of Chinese People's Association for Friendship with Foreign Countries,
Vice President of the Great Wall Society of China

序 ——
景生的牛劲儿

春节前，景生电话说，他昨天又登长城了。我一惊，昨天气温50来年最低，寒潮达极值，山上雪更大，风更猛，天更冷，"你疯啦，这会冻坏的！"他说没事，在山上还迎风对雪，豪咏了毛主席的《沁园春·雪》呢！这口气当属小伙子，可他已67岁了。景生说，近年来凡遇大雪，他总在长城上。

高景生，河北遵化人，是位有成就的知名摄影家，已出版5本大型画册，如今他又在做遵化长城专集。这几年他全身心都扑在了长城上，画册即将出版。我欣赏过景生的长城摄影作品，最近又拜读了他的画册文字及拍摄随笔，收看过他在央视做的长城节目，进一步了解了画册背后的故事，深受感动。

一是勤奋。不入虎穴焉得虎子。景生拍长城不畏艰险，超乎想象，他在2013年7月6日的随笔中写到："长城的松树下，我躺下就打鼾，毕竟六十有五了，连续四天的艰难攀爬，体力严重透支。平山顶山高涧深，长城陡峭，墙土松散，损毁严重，爬起来十分艰险，有时坐在松软的墙脊上前挪，有时四脚并用抓草攀爬，有时荆棘丛中头顶蛛网钻行，两腿酸软，浑身刺痛，战战兢兢，生怕掉进万丈深渊。天黑了，离预定目标还远，只好快快下山。黑暗中我们摸索到8点多钟，才软瘫在山下的面包车中，今天，又攀爬了15个小时。"

"2013.9.1夜困白草洼长城"说："高一声低一声的风，紧一阵慢一阵的雨，慢慢把黑色天幕全拉下来，远远的，稀疏的灯亮了，山山豁豁很快消失在夜幕中。没雨具，没照明，山是下不去了，没有选择，只能在不能栖身的残楼里过夜了。我们钻进透风漏雨的残券洞，不能站，不能靠，不能伸腿，不敢直腰，蜷在残砖上，不知怎么应对这漫漫长夜。只有这一夜，我才真正懂得了什么叫'度日如年'，什么叫'如坐针毡'，什么叫'煎熬'。手机不住地打开，8点35、42、快9点了……就这么一秒秒地看着、熬着。屁股、大腿、老腰、脖子，疼了酸，酸了麻，麻了木，不知是冷还是饿，身子越攒越紧。平日，夜越睡越短，可山上，夜却越熬越长，困神不断袭来，但在冷砖硬瓦一次次磕头撞脑地驱赶下，愣是一夜没睡！"这便是他们所遭磨难的点滴。

二是画外功夫。摄影的功夫在画外。这是毫无疑问的，但往往被忽略。尤其现在，数码相机拿到手没几天就能出"作品"，没多久，又获个什么奖，就成"摄影家"了，乃至忘了天高地厚。这些影友对摄影艺术，只求其表，不去深究。

景生治学严谨，凡事要弄个究竟。他不仅追求影像美，还苦读史书，力求使自己对长城有透彻了解。从春秋战国、秦汉、北齐到明清；从朱元璋、朱棣到戚继光，有关长城的重大事件，他都要了然于胸。生活是本书，他边爬长城边向人请教，山村老叟、村官、羊倌、饭店堂倌……每段长城，每座敌楼，每个关口的历史演变，建筑风格，用料如何，损坏程度，他都有详尽记录或描写。我印象景生风风火火，终日拍片，是个坐不住的人，没想到他能这样静下心来钻研学问。经他实地勘察，匡正了好多以往长城定论中的谬误，如"北齐长城为石垒，明长城为砖砌，后杖子长城能一步越千年"、"遵化长城始于北齐"……景生最欣慰的就是找到了燕长城，他在画册中说："《遵化县志》载：'长城原为燕国所筑。'境内一些如'老马识途'、'三堂坟'等传说也都和燕长城有有关，遵化到底有没有燕长城？有，它又在哪儿呢？经查史，访老，攀崖，终于找到了湮没在锅顶山峰荆棘丛中的'跳石坎'和古烽火台。据判断它正是志书说的、我们要找的燕长城。"

可见，画册不只是本图集，更应有深厚的文化底蕴，融影像与学术性、知识性、趣味性于一体，这是难能可贵的。

三是思考。景生为什么玩儿命拍长城？仅用痴迷摄影是解释不通的。他看到长城的残破感到难过。因年久失修，风浸雨蚀和人为破坏，遵化长城原有敌楼246座，现存较好的仅18座，有的已无踪无影。长城一线铁矿丰富，矿石炙手可热时，长城脚下被弄得乌烟瘴气，有的长城下的山已被掏空了！再就是农民为栽植板栗，滥伐与长城休戚与共的百年松林。景生说登高一望，长城一线十万大山满目疮痍，一片焦黄，惨不忍睹。长城没了保护屏障，空气少了净化器，雾霾日多，干旱缺雨，山土经不住雨水冲刷，用不了多久，就会成为裸山，那时北京周边的生存环境就更脆弱了！每说至此，景生痛心疾首，潸然泪下。景生是个有泪不轻抛的血性硬汉啊。

四是精益求精。讲究影像语言运用。拍照几十年，对摄影语言的运用，光影、色温、构图的把握，应不在话下，但景生却常觉得吃力、苦恼和困惑。他对自己要求很苛刻，随笔中写道："尚存遗憾，留待来日。"许多地方山势凶险，他一去再去，不辞劳苦。我十分喜爱李可染先生的画，尤其是他的牛，为那传神的似与不似间的寥寥数笔，反复推敲，画了再画，呕心沥血，专注至极。

拍风光是用相机作画，道理是相通的。看了景生的长城摄影作品和文字，觉得他颇有一股可染先生画了再画的犟劲儿和先生倡导的忍辱负重、埋头向前的牛劲儿。

最后，我要给景生泼点冷水，再遇春节前那样恶劣天气，就别再登长城了，毕竟年纪不饶人。

蒋铎
高级记者，曾任中国新闻摄影学会副会长

Preface ——
Jingsheng, a Bullheaded Character

Right before the Chinese New Year, Jingsheng called me and told me that on the day before he went to the Great Wall again. I was shocked because the temperature that day plunged to the record low of the past 50 years. Under the polar cold spell, the mountain area must have suffered heavier snow, stronger wind, and lower temperature. "Are you nuts? You are gonna freeze!" He told me that he was fine in the mountains, where he braved the snow storm and chanted spiritedly Chairman Mao's poem "Snow"! He sounded like a young man, but he's already 67. Jingsheng said that in recent years, whenever there was a heavy snow, he happened to be on the Great Wall.

Gao Jingsheng, a native of Zunhua of Hebei Province, distinguished himself as a celebrated photographer. The author of five large-size photography monographs, he is now working on a volume dedicated to Zunhua section of the Great Wall. In recent years, he has fully devoted himself to surveying the Great Wall, and the special volume will soon be published. I enjoy Jingsheng's photography of the Great Wall and his writings along with his photography and his CCTV program on the Great Wall touched me tremendously as I get to further understand the stories behind the book.

The first is the spirit of perseverance. As nothing ventured nothing gained, Jingsheng's courage is beyond imagination when it comes to photographing the Great Wall. His notes written on July 6, 2013 read: "Under a pine tree on the Great Wall, I was totally out at the moment I laid down. Anyhow, at the age of sixty-five, I was truly exhausted after four consecutive days of strenuous climbing. At the peak of Mount Pingshan, the mountains are high and the gullies deep; the Great Wall here is steep with loose and severely damaged rammed-earth wall structure that makes the climbing especially perilous. Sometimes, we inched on our butts along the crumbling crest of the wall; sometimes, we were on all fours and moving along by grabbing grass; sometimes, we had to squeeze ourselves through thorny bushes under spider webs, and end the day with sore legs and aching body that resulted from constant fear of falling into the abyss. When it was getting dark and the targeted destination still beyond reach, we had to turn back and go down reluctantly. In the darkness, we searched our way down the mountains and it was way past 8pm before we collapsed in the van parked at the foothill. Today we made another 15 hours of climbing."

The note of "The night trapped at Baicaowa section of the Great Wall on September 1, 2013" reads: "The howling winds and frenetic rains slowly drew in the nightfall, only sparse lights flickering in the distance. The mountains soon disappeared in the darkness. Without rain gear or lighting tools, there was no way to leave the mountains but to stay at the residual structure that provided very limited shelter. We crawled into a ruined arch gate, where there was no standing space, no place to lean on, to stretch legs or to straighten the body. One could only curl up on a few bricks. I was clueless about how to get through the endless night. It is at that time that I realized what sitting on pins and needles or torment really meant. I kept checking my cell phone, 8:35, 8:42, and almost 9pm... This was how I pulled through the night second by second with a numbing and aching body from neck to buttocks. I could no longer tell whether it was due to the coldness or the hunger that my entire body tightly hunched up. On ordinary days, the night always feels short, but in the mountains the night grows excruciatingly long. Even swamped by weariness, I did not sleep at all as I couldn't hold my head from knocking on the cold hard stone!" So, this is what they have suffered.

The second is a photographer's artistry. The art of photography lies beyond the images, which is without question yet often overlooked. Especially now, those who produce work of art after a few day's playing with digital cameras and win some sort of prize in no time are even entitled photographers. These photographers soon become cocky and only chase after the superficial without delving into the profound.

Jingsheng takes a serious attitude towards his study, and tends to get to the bottom of everything. He not only pursues the beauty of image but also studies history so as to gain a thorough understanding of the Great Wall. Thus, he knows every prominent figure (such as Zhu Yuanzhang, Zhu Di and Qi Jiguang) and all the major events related to the Great Wall throughout the Chinese history, from the Spring and Autumn and Warring States periods, Qin, Han, Northern Qi to Ming and Qing dynasties. Life is a book; on his every trip to the Great Wall, he talked to people along the way, including the elderly in mountain villages, the local administrators, the shepherds, the hotel waiters... He documents the historical development, architectural styles, building materials and degrees of damage of every section of the Great Wall, each watchtower, and each pass in detailed records or description. To me, Jingsheng is always energetic devoting himself to photographing. It is hard to imagine that such an energetic person can settle down and immerse himself in study. His investigation has rectified many misconceptions about the Great Wall, such as that the Great Wall of the Northern Qi dynasty was built of stones, that the Great Wall of the Ming dynasty was built of bricks, that a step on the Houzhangzi section of the Great Wall covers a millennium, and that the Great Wall in Zunhua first appeared in the Northern Qi dynasty. The discovery of the Great Wall dating from the Yan State is the most gratifying moment for Jingsheng. As he remarks in the book: "According to the *Annals of Zunhua County*, the Great Wall, originally built by the Yan State, cradles the story of Santang Tomb as well as such legends as an old horse being a good guide. So, is there a section of the Great Wall built by the Yan State in Zunhua after all? Yes, there is. But where is it? After consulting historical records, interviewing the elderly, and conducting field trips, I finally found the long-lost Tiaoshikan Ridge and the site of the ancient beacon tower among the thorny bushes at the top of Mount Guoding. After verification, they were part of the Yan Great Wall mentioned in the historical records that we had been looking for."

Therefore, a photography album is more an epitome of profound culture than just a collection of photos. It is even more valuable to combine images with knowledge and interest.

The third is an environmentalist's thinking. Why Jingsheng risks his life to photograph the Great Wall? It cannot be explained just by his obsession with photography. He was sad to see the dilapidated Great Wall. Due to disrepair, weathering and human destruction, only 18 of the 246 watchtowers on Zunhua section of the Great Wall are in fair condition of preservation while others have completely gone. The Great Wall sits on top of iron-rich ores. In the prime days of mineral excavation, it was a mess at the foot of the Great Wall. The mountains under some branch walls even have been hollowed out! Then came the farmers, who indiscriminately cut down the pine forests that had been accompanying the Great Wall for hundreds of years just to plant chestnut trees. According to Jingsheng, when viewed afar from a high altitude, the mountainous region along the Great Wall is full of brownish patches, which is really a sad picture. The Great Wall is left standing alone without protective barriers. With less air purifier, more foggy days, frequent droughts and less precipitation, the mountain soil could not withstand the erosion from the rain and the mountains will soon become bare and barren. By then, the environment surrounding Beijing will be more vulnerable! Each time when this becomes the topic, Jingsheng, a tough guy who seldom sheds tears, will be so disheartened that tears well in his eyes.

The fourth is Jingsheng's pursuit for perfection and his carefully wielded scheme of images. With decades of experience in photography, one should have been extremely adept in the use of photographical scheme, the combination of light, shadow and color, as well as picture composition. However, it is not the case for Jingsheng, who is still struggling with the artistic practice, since he sets a very high standard for himself. He once states in his notes: "There are still regrets left for tomorrow." He spares no pains and keeps returning to those precipitous mountain areas. I personally like Li Keran's paintings very much, especially his sketch of cattle, whose spirit is captured in a distorted form with a few lines. This simple sketch is created after repeated drawings, painstaking efforts, and undivided dedication.

Landscape photography is like painting with a camera. The essence of the two is quite similar. Jingsheng's photography and description of the Great Wall remind me of Li's resolute spirit shown in his painting practice and the perseverance he has advocated.

Finally, I would like to make a suggestion to Jingsheng: don't get on the Great Wall again in inclement weather like that on the day before the Chinese New Year. After all, no one can bargain with age.

Jiang Duo

Senior journalist, former Vice President of China Photojournalists' Society

前言——
七年磨一剑 出鞘亮闪闪
——景生，咱的兵没白当

景生是和我携手同日走进军营的战友，从那时起，我们就成了祖国钢铁长城的一块砖。

景生是位摄影艺术家，他的画册《走近清东陵》在平遥国际摄影艺术节上拿了"中国优秀画册"奖后，又把目光盯上了遵化的长城，他要再出一本既能展示气势磅礴、风光无限的家乡长城，又能真实鲜活地反映长城历史、长城文化和长城故事的画册。为这，他心一横，长城一爬就是七年。

这七年，他大山深处苦苦寻找燕长城。历代遵化州志县志都记载"遵化长城始建于燕国"，为证史实，他爬啊，找啊，终于在小厂乡和侯家寨乡境内的悬崖绝顶上找到了断续延绵40多华里的燕长城和燕长城烽火台，并按中国长城学会理事牛泽甫说的"洪山口位于河北省遵化县，约在燕国时建关。"，找到了燕国长城关口——头道城子。景生的发现，匡正了遵化没有燕长城的定论，把遵化长城建筑史向前推进了一千多年，填补了中国长城文化研究的一段空白。

这七年，他醉心于北齐长城文化的研究。他认真阅读北齐长城史，反复勘验舍身台段北齐长城与明长城的差异，发现北齐长城"窄、矮、简、小"。按这一特点，他在马蹄峪与舍身台之间找到了10多段长度不等的北齐长城，并在舍身台西侧发现了北齐长城与明长城交汇的"一步越千年"长城。经他向导，央视"长城内外"摄制组详尽报道了这一长城奇观，并展示了他的长城系列摄影作品。央视一播，舍身台北齐长城和"一步越千年"长城便名声远扬，游人如织。

这七年，他把自己交给了明长城。不管春夏秋冬，无论阴晴雨雪，只要天儿好，他都守在长城上。白草洼峰顶残楼里，他伴着雷电风雨熬过了漫漫长夜；为探雪中沙岭长城，他半个身子掉到了悬崖边……天儿不好时，他就窝在家里钻故纸堆，读明朝史，啃长城书。老伴儿看不过："干脆你撇家舍业跟了长城算了！"

做文化，靠钻研，靠发现，靠细心，更靠坚持。即使是摄影，他也不满足于简单地浮光掠影，而是把所有反映长城历史、长城文化的各种元素符号尽收镜中。他在长城墙体上发现了18块明嘉靖年间（1522—1566）的修城铭文石，把这些铭文汇聚一起，就是一部刻在巨石上的长城活档案。

景生耗时七年，用心血、汗水和智慧为我们绘制了一幅瑰丽恢宏的长城画卷。画卷中，他不仅定格了长城最美的光影瞬间，更融入了自己对长城的赤诚和担当。为成就景生，我愿解囊相助，这既为战友，更是为长城！

景生，咱的兵没白当，长城会记住你，二师会记住你，百姓也会记住你！

韩保平
唐山佰亿售电有限公司 董事长

Preface ——
A Gleaming Sword After Seven Years' Blade-honing
– Jingsheng, Our Days in the Army Are Rewarding

Jingsheng was my comrade-in-arms. We joined the military on the same day. Since then, we have become a brick in the steel-like Great Wall of China, i.e. our motherland.

Jingsheng is a photographer, and his album *Approaching the Eastern Qing Tombs* claimed the award of Chinese Album of Excellence at Pingyao International Photography Festival. After that, he sets his eyes on Zunhua section of the Great Wall and planned to publish another album that will display the magnificent and scenic Great Wall of his hometown on the one hand and illustrate faithfully the history, culture and stories of the Great Wall on the other hand. For this project, he has spent seven years conducting field studies on the Great Wall with unyielding resolution.

In these seven years, he plunged into deep mountains to search for the Yan State Great Wall. Many annals of Zunhua County claim that the Yan State started the construction of the Great Wall in Zunhua. To verify the historical records, Jingsheng searched extensively in the mountain areas and finally found the beacon towers and the ruins of the Yan State Great wall that are scattered in a 20-km long stretch at the cliff top along the borderline of Xiaochang Village and Houjiazhai Township. Based on the statement by Niu Zefu, a member of the Great Wall Society of China, that Hongshan Pass is located in Zunhua County of Hebei Province, and was built in the time of Yan State, Jingsheng found the Pass named Toudao Chengzi. His discovery rectifies the statement that there is no Yan State Great Wall in Zunhua and moves the timeline of the construction history of the Great Wall about one thousand years earlier, filling in a blank in the study of the Great Wall culture.

During these seven years, he was totally engrossed in the study of the Great Wall built in the Northern Qi dynasty. Besides carefully reading the history of the Northern Qi Great Wall, he repeatedly examined and compared the sections of the Great Wall at Sheshen Platform built in the Northern Qi and Ming dynasties, respectively. He discovered that the Northern Qi Great Wall is narrower, lower, simpler, and smaller. Based on these features, he later identified a dozen of remaining sections of various lengths built in this historical period between Mati Valley and Sheshen Platform. He also discovered on the west of Sheshen Platform a section of wall where the Northern Qi Great Wall and Ming Great Wall merged, which made it possible to "cross a millennium in one step". Under his guide, the crew of CCTV's documentary *Inside and Outside the Great Wall* produced a detailed report on the wonder presented by this section of the Great Wall and his series of photographs of the Great Wall. After CCTV's broadcast, the Great Wall of the Northern Qi at Sheshen Platform famous for the view of "crossing a millennium in one step" became widely known and attracted numerous visitors.

In these seven years, he devoted himself to the Ming Great Wall. Regardless of changes of seasons, weather conditions, he stayed on the Great Wall as long as time permitted. In the crumbling architectural ruins at Baicaowa Peak, he spent long nights accompanied by thunders and storms; to explore Shaling section of the Great Wall in snow, he almost fell off the cliff... In the case of extremely bad weather, he stayed at home and buried himself under piles of historical documents, studying history of the Ming dynasty and reading books on the Great Wall. Once his wife was fed up and complained: "Why don't you just give up your family and career and marry to the Great Wall!"

Any cultural mission requires research, discovery, scrutiny, and more importantly, perseverance. Even with photography, Jingsheng is not satisfied with simple and superficial snapshots. Instead, he strives to capture every element and symbol that reflects the history and the culture of the Great Wall. On the wall structure, he found 18 steles with inscriptions about the construction of the wall during Jiajing's reign of the Ming dynasty (1522 - 1566). These inscriptions collectively present a living archive of the Great Wall.

Jingsheng spent seven years in producing a magnificent scroll of the Great Wall, which is a combination of his efforts, sweat and wisdom. In this scroll, he presents us the most enchanting moments of the interplay between light and shadow as well as his appreciation of and dedication to the Great Wall. To support Jingsheng's undertaking, I would like to make a financial contribution, for my fellow warrior as well as for the Great Wall!

Jingsheng, our days in the army are rewarding. People will never forget the contribution you have made to the study of the Great Wall!

Han Baoping

The President of Tangshan Baiyi Electronics Company Ltd.

目录
Contents

遵化长城有几重

遵化长城有几重？这一问，问得人们不免诧异，遵化除了城北罗文峪那道长城，难道还有别的长城？是的，遵化域内除了东起洪山口西至钻天缝那道138华里的明长城外，还有凤凰岭顶上的支墙、宽佃峪关外的重墙、罗文峪关北的土墙、上关湖西山的奇墙和锅顶山峰的圮墙。除支墙和重墙是明长城的附属工事外，其他则应是北齐或更久远的长城了。

How Many Sections of Great Wall Are There in Zunhua

How many sections of Great Wall are there in Zunhua? What a surprising question! Does it mean that there are other sections in Zunhua besides the section at Luowen Valley which is in the north of the city? Yes, in addition to the Great Wall of the Ming dynasty (1368-1644) extending 138 *huali* from Hongshan Pass to Zuantianfeng Crack, there is a branch wall on the top of Fenghuang Ridge, a multi-layered wall outside Kuandianyu Pass, an earthen wall north of Luowenyu Pass, a strange wall on the western hill by Shangguan Lake, and a crumpled wall on the top of Mount Guoding. Except the branch wall and the multi-layered wall, which were auxiliary defense works of the Ming Great Wall, the other walls was probably built in the Northern Qi dynasty or even earlier.

舍身台长城
The Great Wall at Sheshen Platform

上关湖西奇墙
The strange wall on the
western hill by Shangguan Lake

锅顶山上圮墙
The crumpled wall on Mount Guoding

罗文峪关外土墙
The earthen wall
outside Luowenyu Pass

宽佃峪关外重墙
The multi-layered wall
outside Kuandianyu Pass

遵化长城始于燕

公元前663年，齐桓公帮燕国在冀东一带打退入侵的孤竹和令支。之后，遵化大地便有了第一道长城——古老的燕长城。

《遵化州志》、《遵化县志》说遵化长城原为燕国所筑，清人说燕、秦长城皆遵化所必经，《长城印话》说遵化洪山口约在燕国时建关。

The Great Wall of Zunhua Dating from the Yan State Period

After Yan State defeated the invasion of Guzhu State and Lingzhi State in the east of Hebei with the help of the Duke Huan of Qi State in 663BC, Zunhua had its first section of Great Wall built—the ancient Great Wall of Yan.

According to *The Annals of Zunhua Prefecture* and *The Annals of Zunhua County*, Zunhua section of the Great Wall was originally built by the Yan State. Some ancestors in the Qing Dynasty noted that the great walls built by Yan and Qin both passed Zunhua. In *Seal and Word of the Great Wall*, Hongshan Pass in Zunhua was established around the period of the Yan State.

廖家峪长城
The Great Wall at Liaojia Valley

寻找燕长城

遵化历代州志县志关于遵化长城的记载都说"长城原为燕国所筑",清同治十年（1871），遵化州人史朴在《重修遵化城记》中详细记述了遵化境内燕、秦长城的走向："其可取证者，长城当郡治北面，延百数十里，则燕所筑自造阳至襄平、秦所筑自临洮至辽东者，皆所必经，实州境建置，著于史传之始。"

为了验证和延伸遵化长城的历史，崇山峻岭中经三年多艰难而又危险的探寻，2013年12月28日，我们终于找到了湮没在小厂乡境内锅顶山脊的古石墙——"跳石坎"、坍圮在海拔750米高峰上的古烽火台——"老台子"，这也许就是志书和史朴说的燕国长城。

史朴：字文辅，号兰畦，道光丙申进士，署广东肇罗道督粮道，重赴鹿鸣宴，赏二品衔。

Shi Pu, whose courtesy name is Wenfu and elegant name Lanqi, was a *jinshi* (a successful candidate in the palace examination) of 1836 during the reign of Emperor Daoguang, and worked as grain intendant of Zhaoluodao Administrative Garrison (present-day Zhaoqing) in Guangdong. He lived to attend the banquet for new *juren* (a successful candidate in the provincial-level imperial examination) for the second time, and was conferred the second official rank.

A Journey of Exploring the Yan Great Wall

In the annals of both Zunhua Prefecture and Zunhua County throughout the previous ages, it is recorded that the Great Wall was originally built by the Yan State. In the tenth year of the reign of Emperor Tongzhi (1871) in the Qing dynasty, Shi Pu, a native of Zunhua Prefecture, provided details in his book *A Record on the Reconstruction of Zunhua City* about the Great Wall built by Yan and Qin in Zunhua, "Based on available evidences, the Great Wall is located in the north of the county seat, and extends over 100 *li* (50 km). The section built by Yan extended from Zaoyang (close to Dushikou of Hebei Province nowadays) to Xiangping (in Liaoyang of Liaoning Province today), while the one built by Qin ran from Lintao to Liaodong (east of the Liaohe River). Both walls passed Zunhua. The sections of the Great Wall within Zunhua were the first among the establishments of the prefecture that were recorded in historical documents".

To verify and extend the history of the Great Wall in Zunhua, we spent three years on a journey of difficult and dangerous explorations among towering and steep mountains. On December 28, 2013, we finally discovered Tiaoshikan Ridge, which sits in the territory of Xiaochang Township and is the site of an ancient stone wall nestling in the ridges of Mount Guoding and Laotaizi Platform. It is the ruins of an ancient beacon tower on a 750m-high peak. Perhaps they are part of the Great Wall built by Yan State mentioned in the historic annals and by Shi Pu.

右图：罗文峪关外燕长城遗迹
The picture on the right: Remains of the Yan Great Wall outside Luowenyu Pass

寻迹燕长城

In Search of the Great Wall
of the Yan State

作者探寻燕长城遗迹

The author in search of ruins of the Great Wall of the Yan State

头道城子 —— 燕国时的洪山口关

由中国长城学会理事牛泽甫编著、著名长城研究专家罗哲文题写书名的《长城印话》说："洪山口位于河北省遵化县，约在燕国时建关。"书中介绍的"燕国洪山口关"在哪儿呢？顺"跳石坎"、"老台子"所经的锅顶山、刀螂山、牛角山，我们来到了一个叫"头道城子"的山村，《遵化县地名资料汇编》说："长城至此有两道城墙，该村位于第一道城墙附近，故取名头道城子。"按志书、《汇编》和《长城印话》的介绍，这离北面洪山口明长城还有18华里的"第一道城墙"就应该是古老的燕长城了。

如果历代志书、《长城印话》的记载和史朴的记述被重新认定，我们就又找回了被丢弃一千多年的遵化长城史，"跳石坎"、"老台子"以及头道城子原来所在的"燕国关"也就成了遵化历史最悠久、最古老的建筑。燕长城、燕烽火台和燕长城关口的存在和域内大量燕国的历史掌故传说，使得遵化的历史和文化更加厚重悠远，因而也就愈发显得弥足珍贵！

孙志全指点锅顶山燕长城
Sun Zhiquan telling stories about
the Yan Great Wall on Mount Guoding

冯山指点房山沟南梁燕长城
Feng Shan telling stories about
the Yan Great Wall on the
southern mountain range of
Fangshan'gou Village

Toudaochengzi—
Hongshan Pass in the Yan State

According to *Seal and Word of the Great Wall* edited by Niu Zefu, Director of the Great Wall Society of China, and the title of which inscribed by Luo Zhewen, a famous expert on the Great Wall, "Hongshan Pass, located in Zunhua of Hebei, was established around the period of the Yan State." Where is Hongshan Pass of Yan introduced in the book? Walking along Mounts Guoding, Daolang and Niujiao where Tiaoshikan Ridge and Laotaizi Platform are located, we arrived at a village called Toudaochengzi. According to *A Collection of Information about Place Names in Zunhua County*, "There are two walls of the Great Wall here. This village is named Toudaochengzi because it is located near the first wall." According to the annals, *Seal and Word of the Great Wall*, the first Great Wall 18 *huali* from the Ming Great Wall at Hongshan Pass in the north is probably the ancient Great Wall of Yan State.

If the records in the annals of past dynasties and *Seal and Word of the Great Wall* as well as Shi Pu's statement are re-affirmed, we have recovered a history of over 1,000 years for the Great Wall in Zunhua. Tiaoshikan Ridge, Laotaizi Platform and the State of Yan Pass where Toudaochengzi was originally located would prove to be the earliest structures in Zunhua. The presence of the Great Wall, beacon tower and pass dating back to the Yan State period as well as a large number of historical legends of the Yan State in the city enrich the historical and cultural significance of Zunhua, and thus become even more precious!

1. 锅顶山
2. 刀螂山
3. 牛角山
4. 九虎岭
5. 房山岭
6. 寨主沟南山
7. 鹫峰山

1. Mount Guoding
2. Mount Daolang
3. Mount Niujiao
4. Jiuhu Ridge
5. Fangshan Ridge
6. Southern Mountain of Zhaizhu Trench
7. Mount Jiufeng

燕长城经十八盘、锅顶山、刀螂山、牛角山、鹫峰山向西奔去

The Great Wall of the Yan State runs westward via Mounts Shibapan, Guoding, Daolang, Niujiao and Jiufeng.

"跳石坎"和"老台子"

在洪山口明长城南侧的锅顶山至刀螂山山脊上，有道古老的石墙，它与明长城略成直角，经十八盘、锅顶山、刀螂山、牛角山，断断续续地奔鹫峰山而去。山里人要过山脊去迁西必须跨越这道石墙，年长日久，跳来跳去，不知从哪辈子起，老祖宗就叫它"跳石坎"了。在"跳石坎"稍北的锅顶山尖，有一已坍圮成圆鼓鼓大碎石堆的古烽火台，正中舒展展长着一丛灌木，远看好像一巨大丰乳滋润群山，乡亲们都叫它"妈妈头儿"或"老台子"。这道游离于明长城、北齐长城之外，独成体系的古长城和烽火台，各类长城专著从未提起、介绍过它，各路长城专家也未探寻、论证过它，就连曾受它保护过的这块土地上的人们也都慢慢忘却了它的真正身世而淡忘了它。历史是遵化的根，我们是否应按老祖宗"长城原为燕国所筑"的定论，经过考证，认真负责地还"跳石坎"、"老台子"以"燕国长城"的真实身份和名号呢！

Tiaoshikan Ridge and Laotaizi Platform

On the ridge from Mount Guoding to Mount Daolang south of the Ming Great Wall at Hongshan Pass, there is an ancient stone wall, which runs roughly perpendicular to the Ming Great wall. The wall runs disjointedly towards Mount Jiufeng, passing through Mount Shibapan, Mount Guoding, Mount Daolang and Mount Niujiao. To get to Qianxi, people living in the mountains must jump over this stone wall. With the passing of time, people started to call it Tiaoshikan (meaning "jumping over stone ridge"). On the top of Mount Guoding which is a little north to the Tiaoshikan ridge, there is the site of an ancient beacon tower now collapsed into a round pile of debris. In the middle of the debris lies a clump of bushes that appear like a huge plump breast nourishing the surrounding mountains when viewed from afar. Local residents call it Mamatou'er (meaning "mother's breast") or Laotaizi (meaning "old platform"). This section of the ancient Great Wall and the beacon tower form an independent system that lies outside the Ming Great Wall and Northern Qi Great Wall system. However they have never been mentioned or introduced by any work on the Great Wall, nor have they been explored by any experts studying the Great Wall. Even natives of this land who were once protected by the wall have forgotten the original story. History is of tremendous importance to Zunhua. It would be better if we carefully restore the genuine identity and name of the Yan State Great Wall Tiaoshikan, and Laotaizi Platform with textual research and field investigation so as to ascertain the ancestors' conclusion that this Great Wall system was originally built by the Yan State.

锅顶山上燕国烽火台遗址
Ruins of a beacon tower of the Yan State on Mount Guoding

罗文峪关燕长城

罗文峪关有三道长城，一道是横贯东西的明长城，它是遵化九门雄关中的一道大关；一道是关里的重城，是叫做东城、瓮城或鹿圈的南墙；再就是关外约130米的地方，有道从山脚向东直通山脊与明长城汇合的古老残破的长城，这道残城除有10来米的矮小残墙外，其余全是断断续续的石土混合的垄脊。墙体苔迹厚重，用石大小参差不齐，垒石上下不整，完全不像明长城那样巨石垒砌，收顶有度，灰膏勾缝，墙表平整。2014年文物专家考证过这段长城，他们断定不是明长城。是北齐或更久远的长城？专家们没作定论。既然遵化段北齐长城大部分被明长城给叠压了，那么认定这段比鹫峰山北齐长城更显沧桑残老的长城是燕长城似乎就更有说服力了。

有三道城墙的罗文峪关
Luowenyu Pass with three layers of city walls

燕长城
The Yan Great Wall

明长城
The Ming Great Wall

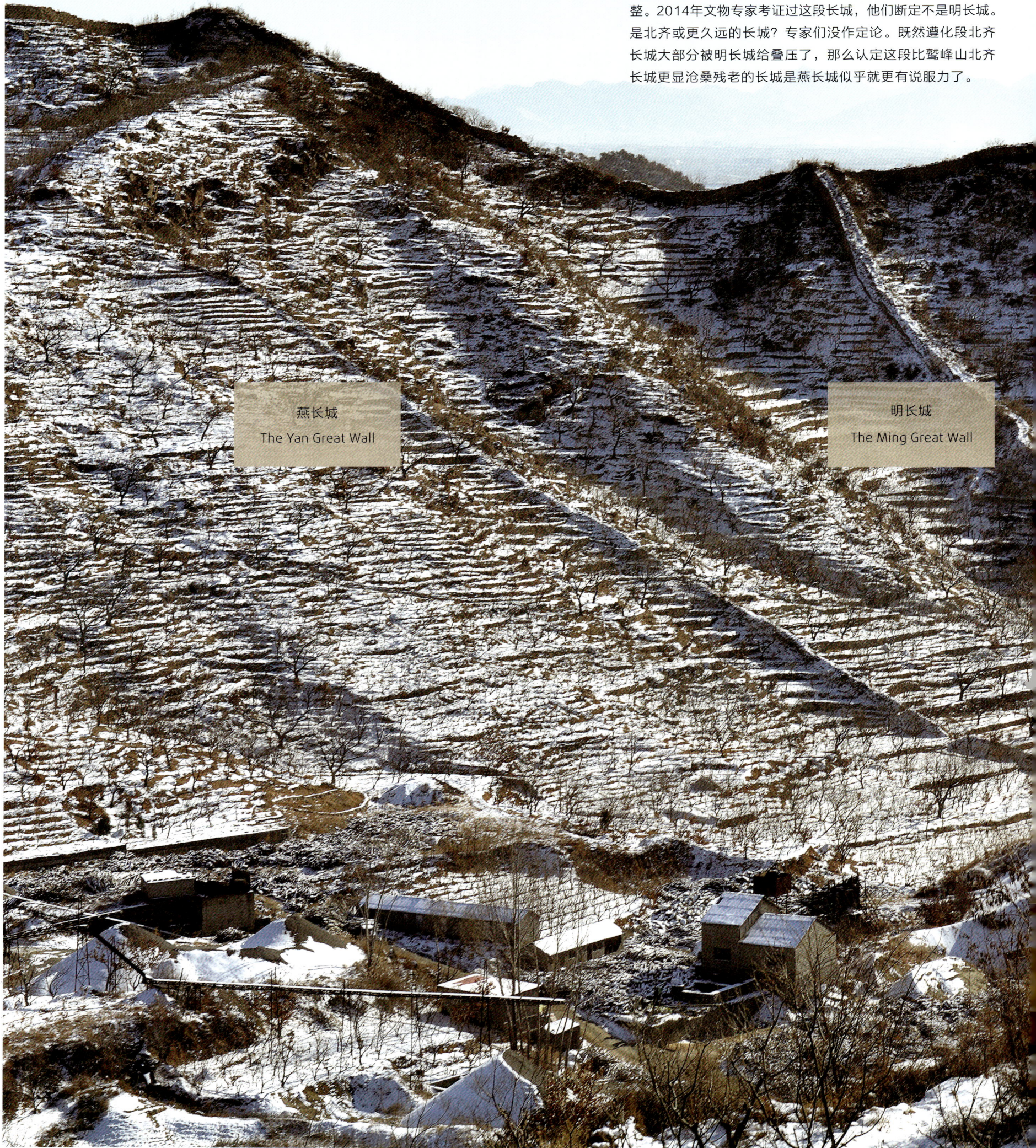

The Yan Great Wall at Luowenyu Pass

There are three sections of the Great Wall at Luowenyu Pass. The first one is the Ming Great Wall running from the east to the west, which forms a major pass of the nine impregnable passes of Zunhua. The second one is the wall within the pass, that is, the Southern Wall of the Eastern City, the barbican or Luquan (Literally meaning "Deer Enclosure"). The third is the ancient and dilapidated Great Wall about 130m outside the pass, which runs eastwards directly through the mountain ridge from the foothill and converges with the Ming Great Wall, consisting of disjointed ridges built with stone-earth mixture except for a short residual wall of about 10m long. Covered with heavy vestiges of mosses, the short wall was built with stones of different sizes and irregular patterns, which is completely different from the Ming Great Wall that was built with rocks of a well-rounded top, plastered joints, and even smooth surface. When archaeologists studied this section of the Great Wall in 2014, they concluded that it was not part of the Ming Great Wall. But they also reached no conclusion whether it is part of the Great Wall of the Northern Qi dynasty or an earlier age. Since most of the Northern Qi Great Wall in Zunhua was overlapped by the Ming Great Wall, it seems more persuasive to say that the section of the Great Wall that looks much more ancient than the Northern Qi Great Wall at Mount Jiufeng is the Yan Great Wall.

明长城重城
The City Wall of
the Ming Great Wall

鲇鱼石关燕长城

上关湖西、明长城北1华里的山顶上，有道416米长、用碎石垒砌的长城和烽火台遗迹，长城墙体上的碎石已被码砌成层层梯田，而烽火台则被拆毁垒成一个似有院墙、通道、战室和两居室模样的特殊工事。当地的乡亲说是刘秀手下大将马武占过这个山头，东边有座山叫"马武坡"，附近还有马武坟（公元25年刘秀曾平流寇于遵化）。从遗址碎石看，它明显有别于巨石垒成的明长城及其附属工事，而北齐长城又被叠压在明长城之下，那这道游离于明长城之外，独成体系的早期长城和烽火台就应当是古老的燕长城了。

The Yan Great wall at Nianyushi Pass

On a peak west of Shangguan Lake and 1 *huali* north of the Ming Great Wall, there are remains of a 416m-long Great Wall and a beacon tower built with gravels. The gravels on the Great Wall have been removed and piled into terraced fields, while the beacon tower has been dismantled to build a special military project seemingly featuring a court wall, a passage, a combat operations room and two bedrooms. Local folks say that this peak was once occupied by General Ma Wu under Liu Xiu, the founding emperor of the Eastern Han dynasty (25-220 AD). On the east there is a mountain called Mawu Slope, near which there is the tomb of Ma Wu. In 25AD, Liu Xiu suppressed roving bandits in Zunhua. The gravels of the remains are obviously different from those of the Ming Great Wall and its auxiliary works that were built with rocks. As the Northern Qi Great Wall was overlapped by the Ming Great Wall, this section of the Great Wall and the beacon tower forming an independent system from the Ming Great Wall are probably part of the ancient Yan Great Wall.

鲇鱼石关外被改造为"巢穴"的燕国烽火台遗址
Remains of the Yan Beacon Tower reconstructed into a "den" outside Nianyushi Pass

遵化何以筑燕城

公元前663年，春秋五霸之一的齐桓公应燕庄公之邀出兵打败了侵犯燕国的令支国王子密卢（《东周列国志》）。燕国将国界从北京一带东扩至迁西、滦县一带，北扩到十八盘至雾峰山一带，为不受侵扰便沿当时的边界修筑了有烽火台和墙体相连的长城，因燕国筑城于燕山也称"燕塞"。这"燕塞"大概就是遵化州志县志所说的燕长城。《热河志》："令

支及孤竹今卢龙、迁安（含迁西）县地，自此以东、北皆戎境……"至燕国全盛时，经大将秦开将边界再东扩至真番、朝鲜，继遵化一带燕长城之后，又修了张家口经多伦、围场至辽阳的燕国最后一道长城。

洪山口长城
The Great Wall at Hongshan Pass

Why Did the State of Yan Build the Great Wall in Zunhua?

In 663 BC, the Duke Huan of Qi State, one of the Five Hegemons of the Spring and Autumn Period (770 BC-476 BC), upon the invitation of the Duke Zhuang of Yan State, dispatched an army to defeat Prince Mi Lu of the Lingzhi State who invaded the Yan State (*The Annals of the Kingdoms in the East Zhou Dynasty*). The Yan State expanded its border from Beijing to Qianxi and Luanxian County in the east and to the area from Mount Shibapan to Mount Jiufeng in the north. To ward off invasions, a great wall with a beacon tower was built along the border then, which is also called Yansai (meaning "Yan's fortification") as the wall was built by the Yan State on the Yanshan Mountains. Yansai is probably the Yan Great Wall recorded in the annals of Zunhua County/Prefecture. *The Annals of the Rehe* records, "Lingzhi and Guzhu are known as Lulong and Qian'an (including Qianxi) today. The areas east and north of this place are territories of Rong..." In the heyday of the Yan State, the border of the state was further expanded eastward to Zhenfan (in Korea today) and Korea. Following the building of the Yan Great Wall of Zunhua, the last section of the Great Wall of the Yan State was built in Zhangjiakou, running through Duolun and Weichang to Liaoyang.

北齐长城舞鹫峰

公元556年（北齐天保七年），北齐筑大同经北京至山海关的长城，遵化的崇山峻岭中便出现了第二道长城——北齐长城。至今，鹫峰山还完好地保存着一段又一段的北齐长城。

The Northern Qi Great Wall at Mount Jiufeng

In 556 AD (the seventh year of the reign of Tianbao of Northern Qi), a section of the Great Wall was built by Northern Qi from Datong, running through Beijing to Shanhai Pass. Thus the second section of the Great Wall appeared among the high mountains of Zunhua—the Northern Qi Great Wall. By far, segments of the Northern Qi Great Wall are still well preserved at Mount Jiufeng.

鹫峰山上北齐长城
The Great Wall at Mount Jiufeng

高洋帝遵化修长城

公元550年，高洋废东魏皇帝继位，国号齐，定都邺，据河南、山西、河北、山东等地，史称北齐。为防柔然、突厥、契丹进攻，六次大修长城，仅公元555年一次就"发夫一百八十万筑城"，还"发寡妇以配军士"。北齐长城的里程稍逊于秦汉长城。就是这样一个被长城包围起来的帝国大厦，仅存28年，传六帝就轰然倒塌了！

Emperor Gao Yang
Built the Great Wall in Zunhua

In 550AD, Gao Yang dethroned the emperor of Eastern Wei (534-550) and established himself as emperor of the State of Qi with its capital in Ye (in present-day Linzhang County). It covered He'nan, Shanxi, Hebei and Shandong and is historically known as the Northern Qi Dynasty. To prevent the attacks of Rouran, Turkish and Khitan tribes, Gao Yang built the Great Wall six times. In 555AD alone, "1.8 million men were summoned to build the wall", and "widows were dispatched to be wives of soldiers". The mileage of the Northern Qi Great Wall was only a little less than the Great Wall of Qin and Han. However, the state of Qi, which was enclosed by the Great Wall lasted only 28 years and collapsed in the reign of its sixth emperor!

鹫峰山北齐长城
The Great Wall at Mount Jiufeng

鹫峰山北齐长城
The Great Wall at Mount Jiufeng

鳌峰山北齐长城
The Great Wall at Mount Jiufeng

长城精品——
鹫峰山上北齐城

遵化市鹫峰山旅游风景区舍身台往北、往西有段所谓"最窄的长城"，只要你驻足细看，就会发现这段长城与我市其他长城截然不同，通高不过3米，顶部平整，最窄处只70厘米，没垒巨石，没勾灰膏，没设垛口，没有其他附属工事，符合北齐长城窄、矮、小、简特点，是域内唯一没被明长城湮埋的北齐长城。在风景区，又保存得这么完好的北齐长城，在万里长城中实为罕见，是难得的长城精品。这段完好的北齐长城为啥未被明长城替代？这里峰高壁险，不通大川，易守难攻，所以务实的蓟镇第38任总兵成勋才未劳师动众再加叠修，给鹫峰山至马蹄峪关留下了一段难得的北齐长城。硬把它说成是蓟镇第48任总兵戚继光为保护环境和寺庙而手下留情，那就张冠李戴、亵渎历史了。

Rare Remains of the
Great Wall at Mount Jiufeng

Towards the north and the west of Sheshen Platform, there is the so-called narrowest section of the Great Wall. A close look of the wall will reveal that this section is completely different from other sections of the Great Wall in Zunhua. It is less than 3m tall, has an even top and, is only 70cm wide at its narrowest part. It was built without using any huge rocks, plaster joints or crenels, and has no auxiliary work, which meet the characteristics of the Northern Qi Great Wall of being narrow, low, small and simple. It is the only section of the Northern Qi Great Wall not replaced by the Ming Great Wall in Zunhua. Throught the entire Great Wall of China, it is really rare to see a section as well preserved as the section of the Northern Qi Great Wall in this scenic area. Why wasn't this section replaced by the Ming Great Wall? Here, with lofty peaks and precipitous cliffs and no big rivers, it is easy to defend and difficult to attack. Therefore, Cheng Xuncai, the 38th Commander-in-Chief of Jizhen Garrison (present-day Jizhou District) didn't order the people to rebuild the wall, thus leaving a rare section of the Northern Qi Great Wall extending from Mount Jiufeng to Matiyu Pass. It would be a violation of history to say that this section was retained as a result of the mercy of Qi Jiguang, the 48th Commander-in-Chief of Jizhen Garrison, to protect the environment and temples.

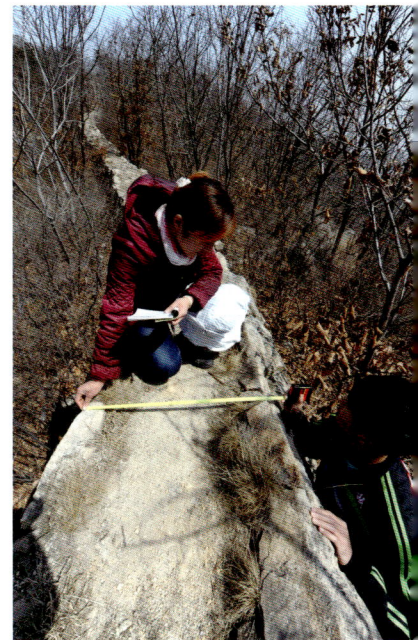

鹫峰山北齐长城最窄处仅70厘米
The narrowest section of the
Northern Qi Great Wall at Mount Jiufeng
is only 70cm in width

鹫峰山上有看点　　脚下一步越千年

当你从舍身台烽火台的北侧，顺窄小坍圮的北齐长城西行约100米时，眼前会突然出现宽阔的马道和外侧隆起的勾灰石垛墙，常走长城的人都知道这宽大高耸的石墙，正是嘉靖三十年后修建的明朝石长城。"呀，怎么只这一步就从北齐长城迈到明长城上来了！"是的，在北齐长城与明长城的交汇处，从北齐天保七年（556）到明朝嘉靖四十五年（1566），您这一步真的迈出了一千多年呢！

北齐长城和明长城交汇处

The intersection of the Northern
Qi Great Wall and the Ming Great Wall

Take One Step to Traverse 1,000 Years at Mount Jiufeng

When you walk westward for about 100m from the northern side of Sheshen Platform Beacon Tower along the narrow and collapsed Northern Qi Great Wall, you will suddenly see a wide riding track with an external plastered battlement. People who often walk on the Great Wall know that this wide and lofty stone wall is a stone great wall of the Ming dynasty built after the thirtieth year of the reign of Emperor Jiajing. "Ah, how come that one step takes me from the Northern Qi Great Wall to the Ming Great Wall!" Yes, at the intersection of the Northern Qi Great Wall and the Ming Great Wall, one step really traverses 1,000 years from the 7th year of the reign of Emperor Tianbao of Northern Qi (556AD) to the 45th year of the reign of Emperor Jiajing of Ming dynasty (1566AD)!

"罗文"、"月娥"无觅处，
隋唐遵化已设关

长城关口罗文峪，说是因隋朝武将罗文守关而始名。查罗氏族谱，隋朝没有罗文其人，更无武将可言。说洪山口是因洪月娥守城而名，还说罗章在此跪楼搬兵，更是个张冠李戴的讹传。志载也好，民传也罢，都证明了一个不争的事实，早在隋唐遵化长城已经设关戍守（《长城印话》说洪山口燕时已设关）。自北齐之后，北周（557—581）大象初年大将诏翼提"创新改旧"，督修遵化等段长城；隋开皇元年（581）幽州总管阴寿击败来犯的高宝宁后"缘边修保障，竣长城……"督修了遵化等段长城。隋后的唐、宋、辽、元等几百年，长城基本未动过土石，直到大明王朝建立后，工程浩瀚的万里长城重修帷幕才又徐徐拉开。

No Traces of Luo Wen and Yue'e to be Found, Yet the Pass Already There in Zunhua in Sui and Tang Dynasties

The pass in Luowen Valley along the Great Wall is said to be named after Luo Wen, a general of the Sui dynasty stationed there. Actually, no one with the name of Luo Wen has been discovered in the family tree of Luo in the Sui dynasty, let alone a general. It is even more groundless to say that Hongshan Pass was named after Hong Yue'e who defended the city and that Luo Zhang called for assistance by kneeling at the city gate. However, both the historical records and folklores reveal an indisputable fact that Zunhua section of the Great Wall was garrisoned as early as in the Sui and Tang dynasties, and *Seal and Word of the Great Wall* even reads that Hongshan Pass was set up as early as in the Yan State period. After the Northern Qi dynasty, in the first year of Daxiang period of the Northern Zhou dynasty (557-581), General Zhao Ji proposed "innovation and reform" and supervised the restoration of sections of the Great Wall in Zunhua and other places. In the first year of Emperor Kaihuang of Sui (581AD), Yin Shou, Governor of Youzhou (present-day Beijing, Tianjin, and some places in north Hebei), built fortresses and the Great Wall along the border after he defeated the invasion led by Gao Baoning, and supervised the restoration of the Great Wall in Zunhua and other places. During several hundred years from Sui to Tang, Song, Liao and Yuan dynasties, basically no work was done on the Great Wall until the gradual start of the reconstruction of the Great Wall since the establishment of the Ming dynasty.

听罗文峪久远的故事
Listen to the age-long story
of Luowen Valley

龙伏东来明长城

公元1368年，朱元璋建立大明王朝，开启了270多年的长城大修帷幕，北齐长城之上，遵化又矗起了一道巍峨于世的明长城。

遵化长城主要是明长城，为开国大将徐达沿北齐长城创修，经洪武、永乐、成化、弘治、嘉靖、隆庆、万历等朝屡加修建，特别是经戚继光16年的大规模修筑，遵化才有了这轰动世界的壮阔奇观。

The Awe-inspiring Ming Great Wall Extending Like a Dragon

In 1368, Zhu Yuanzhang founded the Ming dynasty, initiating the major restoration of the Great Wall lasting over 270 years. On the Northern Qi Great Wall, a lofty section of the Ming Great Wall was erected in Zunhua.

Zunhua section of the Great Wall was mainly built under the leadership of the Ming-dynasty founding general Xu Da along the Northern Qi Great Wall. It has been further developed throughout the reigns of Hongwu, Yongle, Chenghua, Hongzhi, Jiajing, Longqing and Wanli emperors in the Ming dynasty. In particular, the 16-year large-scale building and repair by Qi Jiguang brought the world-renowned spectacular wonder to Zunhua.

石崖岭寨长城
The Great Wall at Shiyaling Stockaded Village

洪武置卫

洪武六年（1373）朱元璋派徐达戍守长城边务，又从淮安侯华云龙言，"在永平、蓟州、密云以西二千余里长城的一百二十九个关隘处，皆置戍守（含遵化）"。洪武十一年（1378）设遵化卫（卫为军事组织，一卫统5600兵）。洪武十五年（1382）从北平都司言，在燕山一线的……洪山口、刁山寨、马蹄峪、蔡家峪、秋科峪、甘查峪、罗文峪、猫儿峪、山寨峪、挞角山、沙坡峪、山口寨、冷嘴头、龙池寨、大安口、井儿峪、琵琶峪、鲇鱼石、平山寨、马兰峪、峰台岭、宽佃峪、饿老婆顶……凡二百处，各卫校卒戍守其地。至此，北平以东长城各关隘防御体系基本完成。

后杖子长城
The Great Wall at Houzhangzi Village

Zunhua Wei Military Unit Was Established in the Hongwu Reign

In the sixth year of the Hongwu reign (1373), Zhu Yuanzhang dispatched Xu Da to garrison the Great Wall and also ordered via the Marquis of Huai'an, or Hua Yunlong, "All the 129 passes along the Great Wall extending over 2,000 *li* which is in the west of Yongping, Jizhou and Miyun shall be garrisoned (including Zunhua)." In the 11th year of Hongwu reign (1378), Zunhua Wei (wei was a military unit consisting of 5,600 soldiers) was established. In the 15th year of Hongwu reign (1382), Zhu Yuanzhang ordered from the Beiping Dusi, or Beiping Regional Military Commission, that 200 places along the Yanshan Mountains, should all be garrisoned including Hongshan Pass, Diaoshan Stockaded Village, Mati Valley, Caijia Valley, Qiuke Valley, Gancha Valley, Luowen Valley, Mao'er Valley, Shanzhai Valley, Mount Wojiao, Shapo Valley, Shankou Stockaded Village, Lengzuitou Pass, Longchi Stockaded Village, Da'an Pass, Jing'er Valley, Pipa Valley, Nianyushi Pass, Pingshan Stockaded Village, Malan Valley, Fengtai Ridge, Kuandian Valley, and Elaopo Peak… By far, the defense system for all passes of the Great Wall in the east of Beiping had been basically completed.

徐达筑关

朱元璋于1368年率军攻克元大都（北京）建立明王朝，元顺帝虽败走漠北但实力依然强大，朱元璋说："惟西北胡世患中国，不可不备。"为防残元侵扰，洪武十四年（1381）徐达在北齐长城冲要处修关筑隘。"辛酉，征虏大将军魏国公徐达发燕山等卫屯兵万五千一百人修永平界岭等三十二关。"（《永平府志·关隘》）遵化境内修筑了洪山口、西安峪、白枣峪、三道岭、马蹄峪、秋科峪、甘查峪、罗文峪、猫儿峪、山寨峪、沙坡峪、山口寨、石崖岭、马兰关等14个关隘。于是，遵化长城便成了北齐墙、明朝关的混合防御工事。

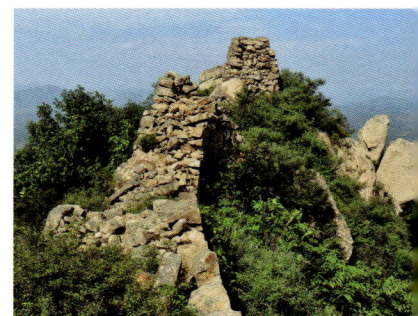

天胜寨长城
The Great Wall at
Tiansheng Stockaded Village

Xu Da Built Passes

In 1368, Zhu Yuanzhang led his army to conquer the capital of the Yuan dynasty (Beijing) and established the Ming dynasty. Emperor Shun of Yuan dynasty was still powerful despite his defeat and exile in the northern deserts. Zhu Yuanzhang said, "We cannot afford to ignore the perils of barbarian invasion of the Central Plains from the northwest." To prevent the invasion and harassment of residual Yuan forces, in the 14th year of the Hongwu reign (1381), Xu Da built passes at strategically important places of the Northern Qi Great Wall. "In 1381, Xu Da, Duke of Wei and Zhenglu General (lit. "General Who Attacks Barbarians"), dispatched 15,100 soldiers stationed in the Yanshan Mountains and other places to build 32 passes including the Yongpingjie Ridge" (*Passes* in *The Annals of the Yongping Prefecture*). A total of 14 passes were built within Zunhua, including Hongshan Pass, Xi'an Valley, Baizao Valley, Sandao Ridge, Mati Valley, Qiuke Valley, Gancha Valley, Luowen Valley, Mao'er Valley, Shanzhai Valley, Shapo Valley, Shankou Stockaded Village, Shiya Ridge and Malan Pass. As a result, Zunhua section of the Great Wall became mixed defensive works consisting of Northern Qi walls and Ming passes.

三道岭寨长城
The Great Wall at Sandaoling Stockaded Village

永乐增关

继洪武十四年（1381）遵化构筑14个关寨后，永乐年间又构筑了天胜寨、舍身台、蔡家峪、冷嘴头、龙池寨、大安口、井儿峪、琵琶峪、沙岭儿、鲇鱼石、平山寨、龙洞峪、宽佃峪等13个关寨，加上弘治十三年（1500）构筑的独松峪、峰台岭，正德三年（1508）构筑的廖家峪，正德十年（1515）构筑的饿老婆顶寨，遵化138华里的长城上前后共构筑了31个关寨。

New Passes Were Built in the Yongle Reign

Following the construction of 14 passes in Zunhua in 1381, 13 passes were added during the reign of Emperor Yongle, including Tiansheng Stockaded Village, Sheshen Platform, Caijia Valley, Lengzuitou Pass, Longchi Stockaded Village, Da'an Pass, Jing'er Valley, Pipa Valley, Shaling'er Valley, Nianyushi, Pingshan Stockaded Village, Longdong Valley, and Kuandian Valley,. In addition to Dusong Valley, and Fengtailing Pass built in the 13th year of the Hongzhi reign (1500), Liaojiayu Pass built in the third year of the reign of Zhengde (1508), and Elaopo Peak Stockaded Village built in the tenth year of the reign of Zhengde (1515), 31 passes and stockaded villages were built along Zunhua section of the Great Wall extending 138 *huali*.

"土木堡之变"和遵化长城

正统十四年（1449）英宗皇帝在太监王振怂恿下，亲统50万大军北征瓦剌（蒙古部落），被瓦剌三万军队在土木堡（今张家口市怀来境内）打得落花流水，皇帝被俘，长城重创，若不是兵部尚书于谦率众死守京师，中国历史或就此被改写，史称"土木堡之变"。事变后驻遵化的顺天巡抚、右佥都御史邹来学上疏"广斥堠，谨烽燧，储财用，举将才，守要害，精兵械"，并督修遵化等京东长城。遵化建"邹公祠"以祀。代宗、英宗多次下令加修遵化一线长城；成化十二年（1476）蓟镇总兵李铭督修遵化等段长城；弘治朝，巡抚顺天、整饬蓟州边备、右副都御史洪钟缮复含遵化境内等处城堡270所。

Tumu Fort Crisis and Zunhua Section of the Great Wall

In the 14th year of Zhengtong (1449), Emperor Yingzong, instigated by Eunuch Wang Zhen, led a huge army of 500,000 soldiers in a northern expedition to Wala (a Mongol tribe), only to be utterly routed by Wala's troops of 30,000 soldiers at the Tumu Fort (within present-day Huailai county of Zhangjiakou City), with the emperor captured and the Great Wall heavily damaged. The Chinese history would have been altered had the Minister of War Yu Qian not led the people to defend the capital city to the last. This is called the Tumu Fort Crisis in history. Zou Laixue, Shuntian Grand Coordinator and Imperial Censor in Zunhua after the crisis, presented a memorial to the throne, "We should set up many watchtowers, carefully use beacon towers, save financial resources, recommend talented militarists, guard strategic positions and manufacture advanced weapons." Meanwhile, he supervised the repair of sections the Great Wall in places east of the capital such as Zunhua. The Temple of Duke Zou was built in Zunhua. Emperor Daizong and Emperor Yingzong issued several orders to rebuild the frontier Great Wall in Zunhua. In the 12th year of Chenghua reign (1476), Commander-in-Chief Li Ming at Jizhen Garrison supervised the renovation sections of the Great Wall in places like Zunhua. In the reign of Hongzhi, Shuntian Grand Coordinator and Censor Hong Zhong restored 270 forts within the territory of Zunhua.

山寨峪长城
The Great Wall at Shanzhai Valley

"庚戌之变"和遵化长城

嘉靖二十九年（1550）俺答率十万蒙古大军围困京师，严嵩戒兵部坚壁勿战，不发一矢。俺答在京外及山西、河北一带焚烧饱掠八日方退，史称"庚戌之变"。为保京师安全，提督孙桧上疏："蓟州一带边墙、隘口、堡寨、墩台，特别残缺。"总督何栋上疏："自山海关至居庸关……应修边墙，并铲崖。"嘉靖三十年（1551）遵化开始大规模创修、复修长城；嘉靖三十六年（1557）鞑靼逼近遵化、迁安等处，严嵩提"须将各口原修未竟边墙，作速修补坚固"，于是遵化长城又进行了多处修复。

The Gengxu War and Zunhua Section of the Great Wall

In the 29th year of the Jiajing reign (1550), Altan Khan led a Mongol army of 100,000 soldiers to besiege the capital city. Yan Song forbad the Minister of War from fighting, ordering them not to shoot an arrow. Altan Khan didn't retreat until after eight days of burning and plundering outside Beijing and along Shanxi and Hebei. This is called the Gengxu War in history. To ensure the safety of the capital, provincial commander-in-chief Sun Hui presented a memorial to the throne, pointing out that "the side walls, mountain passes, stockaded villages and abutments along the Jizhou Prefecture are especially dilapidated." Governor He Dong presented a memorial that "border walls should be rebuilt and some cliffs should be cut off from the Shanhai Pass to Juyong Pass...." In the 30th year of Jiajing reign (1551), large-scale construction and reconstruction of the Great Wall were started in Zunhua. In the 36th year of Jiajing reign, as Tartars drew near Zunhua, Qian'an and other places, Yan Song proposed to "rapidly repair and reinforce border walls not completed at various passes." As a result, several places of the Zunhua section of the Great Wall were repaired and renovated.

罗文峪长城
The Great Wall at Luowen Valley

万里长城称"边"不是"边"

明朝立国后，朱元璋于洪武三年至二十五年（1370—1392）五次北伐，把领地推到了蒙古腹地和林（今蒙古国哈尔和林）等地，并在蒙古边境一带设东胜、大宁等40余个卫所，形成了防御蒙古南侵的第一道防线，称"外边"；而东起鸭绿江、西抵嘉峪关的万里长城，其实是呵护中原和京城的第二道防线，称"内边"。朱棣"靖难之役"借助蒙古兀良哈三卫于1403年打败朝廷夺位登基。作为回报，将东胜、大宁拱手让给兀良哈，致使明朝北部边防出了两个大口子，后来北疆防线终于退到了现在的明长城，明长城也由"内边"变成了"外边"。为加强防守，自永乐七年（1409）起，沿长城先后设置了辽东、蓟州、宣府、大同、山西、延绥、固原、宁夏、甘肃九个军事重镇，史称"九边"（居庸关至山海关为蓟镇长城）。

凤凰岭长城
The Great Wall at Fenghuang Ridge

The Great Wall, Called a "Border", Is Not a "Border"

Following the establishment of the Ming dynasty, Zhu Yuan-zhang conducted five expeditions northward from the 3rd to the 25th year of the Hongwu reign (1370-1392), extending his territory to Helin (present-day Kharkhorin of Mongol) in the interior land of Mongol, and set up over 40 garrisons in Dongsheng and Daning along the region bordering Mongol, forming the first line of defense against the southern invasion of Mongol known as the Outer Border. The Great Wall, extending from the Yalu River in the east to Jiayu Pass in the west was actually the second line of defense protecting the Central Plains and the capital city, which is called the Inner Border. During the Jingnan Campaign, with the assistance of the three *wei* military units of the Uriankhai in Mongol, Zhu Di defeated the court to ascend the throne in 1403. In return, Zhu Di surrendered Dongsheng and Daning to Uriankhai, resulting in two big openings in the northern border of the Ming dynasty. Later the northern border defense force finally retreated to the present Ming Great Wall, which was turned from an Inner Border into an Outer Border. To strengthen border defense, from the 7th year of the Yongle reign (1409), nine military garrisons were established along the Great Wall, namely, Liaodong, Jizhou, Xuanfu, Datong, Shanxi, Yansui, Guyuan, Ningxia and Gansu, known as Nine Border Garrisons in history (the section extending from Juyong Pass to Shanhai Pass was Jizhen Garrison section of the Great Wall).

琵琶峪长城
The Great Wall at Pipa Valley

长城的建造

长城奔腾于崇山峻岭之上。巨大的基石，厚重的青砖，众多的土方是怎样运上山巅，垒砌成墙的呢？

以险制塞

万里长城大多建于崇山峻岭的山脊之上，而关隘多建于两山夹口和河谷汇合回转处，这样既以险拒敌，又节省巨大的人力物力。

就地取材

长城的建材大都修到哪取到哪，石料用土取自就近固定的石、土场，不漫山遍野乱采滥挖，灰、砖就地烧造。如我市的北窑、双窑、北窑厂、张家窑都是当年为长城烧砖瓦烧石灰的地方。建材由人工和畜力搬运，修明长城时已有了简单的机械搬运。

兵夫并用

修长城的劳力来源：一是戍边将士，他们边戍守，边屯田，边修城，工程巨大而民怨不大。二是强征民夫，秦始皇强征五十万民夫修城九年；北齐皇帝征发一百八十万民夫修城，男丁征尽，连寡妇都征来修城，民怨沸腾。三是充军犯人，秦汉时专门有一种刑罚叫"城旦"，就是罚修长城的犯人。明修长城也使用了大量犯人，把刑期折合成工程量，完工即释放。军夫是明修长城的主要人工来源。

分包工程

长城的修筑多采用分段包干的办法，把某段墙体、某座敌台、某个关隘分包给某营、某卫所，再下分给戍卒、囚犯和募夫。由总督、巡抚、经略、总兵官督理，千总、把总等具体组织实施。

The Construction of the Great Wall

The Great Wall runs over high mountains and lofty hills. How were the huge cornerstones, heavy gray bricks and so much earth carried to the mountain tops and built into walls?

Precipitous positions were chosen to build stockades
Most parts of the Great Wall were built on the ridges of high mountains, while strategic posts were mostly constructed at passes between two mountains and the bends of river valleys. In this way, not only were precipitous positions leveraged to resist enemies, but also tremendous human and material resources were saved.

Local materials were used
Building materials for the Great Wall were obtained wherever the wall was being built. Stones and earth were from nearby fixed stone and earth fields instead of being mined without regulations. Lime and bricks were fired nearby. For example, the Beiyao Kiln, the Shuangyao Kiln, the Beiyao Workshop and the Zhangjia Kiln were places for firing bricks, tiles and lime during the time when the Great Wall was being built. Building materials were carried by manual and animal labor, and simple mechanical transport tools were available when the Ming Great Wall was being built.

Both soldiers and conscripted workers were involved
Labor sources for the building of the Great Wall: The first source was soldiers garrisoning frontiers. They defended the border and reclaimed fields while building the Great Wall, and didn't cause major popular discontent despite the huge amount of work. The second source was forced conscripted workers. Emperor Qin Shi Huang forced 500,000 conscripted workers to build the Great Wall for nine years. The emperor of the Northern Qi dynasty forced 1.8 million conscripted workers to build the wall and even forced widows to work on the wall when men were exhausted, causing great discontent from the public. The third source was criminals deported to build the Great Wall for penal servitude. During the Qin and Han dynasties, there was a punishment called *chengdan*, meaning being sentenced to build the Great Wall. A large amount of criminals were also involved in building the wall in the Ming dynasty. With their term of imprisonment converted into certain amount of work, they would be released once their work was done. Military workers were the main labor source for the building of the Great Wall in the Ming dynasty.

Subcontracted work
Subcontracting was adopted for the building of most sections of the wall. That is, a certain section of wall, a certain watchtower, or a certain pass was subcontracted to a certain garrison or *weisuo* military unit, and was then further subcontracted to soldiers, prisoners or conscripted workers. Governor-generals, grand coordinators, lieutenants and commander-in-chief were in charge of supervision, while brigade commander or squad leaders in charge of or ganization and implementation.

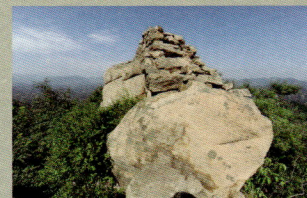
天胜寨长城
The Great Wall at Tiansheng Stockaded Village

万寿庵明长城砖窑遗址
Ruins of a brick kiln of the Ming Great Wall at Wanshou Nunnery

刻有"遵化卫迤西一十二丈雇募夫修"的界石
A boundary stone with an inscription meaning "the wall 12 *zhang* (40m) west of Zunhua Garrison was built by hired workers"

后杖子明长城砖石垛口交汇处
The brick crenel junction of the Ming Great Wall at Houzhangzi Village

基石　Cornerstone
箭窗　Embrasure
敌台　Watchtower
铺房　Duty room
拱门　Archway
雷石孔　Grenade hole
宇墙　Short wall parallel with a crenel

箭鱼石长城
The Great Wall at Nianyushi Pass

垛口
crenel

便门
Side door

望孔
Watch hole

长城防御工事和防御系统

明长城的防御工事分为镇城、路城、营城、关城、城墙、敌台、墙台、烽火台、拦马沟和拦马墙。它们相互联系，相互配合，共同组成一个完整的防御工程体系，关城极冲。敌台筑有基石，设有券室，建有楼橹，环有垛口，是可供瞭望戍守、贮藏军械粮草的堡垒。明长城的军事防御体系为兵部（兵部尚书）——镇（总兵，将士十万人）——路（参将、游击将军）——营（提调）——关（千总）——敌台（把总率二三十人把守）。

The Defense Works and the Defense System of the Great Wall

The defense works of the Ming Great Wall consisted of garrisons of *zhencheng* (where the head of a garrison was stationed), *lucheng* , *yingcheng*, and *guancheng*, city walls, watchtowers, wall units, beacon towers, horse blocking trenches, and horse blocking walls. They were connected and coordinated with each other to jointly form a complete defense work system, of which passes bore the brunt. A watchtower has footstones and arch rooms, and is surrounded by crenels, which is an abutment for keeping a lookout and defense and storing weapons and grains. The military defense system of the Ming Great Wall consisted of the Ministry of War (headed by the Minister of War), *zhen* (headed by commander-in-chief with 100,000 soldiers), *lu* (headed by *canjiang*, or "staff general" and brigade commander), *ying* (headed by an inspector), *pass* (headed by brigade commander) and watchtower (guarded by 20-30 soldiers headed by squad leader).

❶ 一等边墙
——双面砖包墙（洪山口长城）

First-class side wall
—double-sided brick-covered wall (the Great Wall at Hongshan Pass)

❷ 二等边墙
——单面砖包墙（白枣峪长城）

Second-class side wall
—single-sided brick-covered wall (the Great Wall at Baizao Valley)

❸ 三等边墙
——砖垛口墙（后杖子长城）

Third-class side wall
—brick-crenel wall (the Great Wall at Houzhangzi Village)

❹ 四等边墙
——石垛口墙（后杖子长城）

Fourth-class side wall
—stone-crenel wall (the Great Wall at Houzhangzi Village)

❺ 五等边墙
——山险墙（马蹄峪长城）

Fifth-class side wall
—precipitous mountain wall (the Great Wall at Mati Valley)

❶ 砖垛墙和砖马道
Brick crenel wall and brick riding track

❷ 长城敌台通顶楼梯
The staircase leading to the top of a watchtower

❸ 石马道
Stone horse-riding track

❹ 人工垒砌的拦马墙
Man-made horse-blocking wall

❺ 战台（马面）
War platform (horse face)

❻ 长城内侧便门
Side door on the Great Wall

❼ 砖望孔
Brick watch hole

❽ 回廊式敌台
Corridor-styled watchtower

❾ 炮架支孔
Cannon support hole

❿ 雷石孔
Stone hole

戚继光变"静态长城"为"动态长城"

戚继光驻三屯营总兵府镇边十六年，爬山涉险，实地勘察，在全面扩建改建重建蓟镇长城墙体、关城、城堡、墙台、哨墙、铺房、烽墩等一系列配套军事设施的基础上，还借鉴弘治年间延绥巡抚文贵砖木空墩做法，在蓟镇长城上发明创建了1337个既可戍守贮藏，又能对敌作战的空心敌台，将古长城防御体系由"静态阻隔"为主，转向"动态作战"为主，使长城由"战略长城"变成了"战术长城"，创造了古代军事史和建筑史上的奇迹。戚继光在把和平安宁带给关里百姓的同时，还为中华民族留下了一大笔宝贵的物质财富和精神财富。

Qi Jiguang Turned a "Static Great Wall" into a "Dynamic Great Wall"

Qi Jiguang held the post of Commander-in-Chief of Santun Garrison for 16 years. During this period, he ventured to make field explorations among precipitous mountains to comprehensively expand and reconstruct a series of supporting military facilities such as the walls, passes, towers, platforms, sentry walls, wall units with a room, and beacon towers of Jizhen Garrison section of the Great Wall. On the basis of that, he inventively build 1,337 hollow watchtowers that could not only defend the enemy, store weapons and grains, but also combat with the enemy drawing on Grand Coordinator Wen Gui's practice of building brick-timber hollow abutments during the reign of Hongzhi. As a result, the ancient Great Wall defensive system was turned from mainly static blocking to dynamic fighting, and the Strategic Great Wall was transformed into the Static Great Wall, presenting a miracle in the ancient military and architectural history. While bringing peace and stability to people within the Great Wall, Qi Jiguang also left a valuable material and spiritual legacy to the Chinese nation.

廖家峪长城
The Great Wall at Liaojia Valley

戚继光（1527—1587）：明朝抗倭名将、军事家。字元敬，号南塘，又号孟渚。山东登州（今山东蓬莱）人。戚继光在蓟镇十六年，加固长城，筑建墩台，整顿屯田，训练军队，制订车、步、骑配合作战的战术，形成墙、台、堑密切联络的防御体系，多次击退侵扰之敌，军威大振，蓟门平静。时人誉之为"足称震古之名将，无愧万里之长城"。

Qi Jiguang, born in 1527 and died in 1587, is a famous general and militarist known for leading the fight on the coastal regions against pirate activities in the Ming dynasty. His courtesy name is Yuanjing and art names are Nantang and Mengzhu. And he is a native of Dengzhou of Shandong (Penglai of Shandong today). During his 16 years' work in the Jizhen Garrison, he reinforced the Great Wall, built abutments, regulated garrison troops' reclamation of wasteland, trained the army, formulated a tactic of coordinated fighting with chariot soldiers, infantry and cavalry, and created a defense system with close contact between walls, towers and moats. After several defeats of invading enemies, the military might of the Ming dynasty was greatly reinvigorated, and the area around the Ji Prefecture became peaceful. He was acclaimed by people of his time as "being worthy of the fame of an eminent general outshining all ancient ones, and worthy of the prestige of the Great Wall of 10,000 *li*."

洪山口长城
The Great Wall at Hongshan Pass

戚继光修座敌台要花多少钱？

隆庆六年（1572）戚继光督修的第一期工程结束，蓟、昌两镇共修1206座敌台。若民修，一座敌台600至1000两银子也难修成，而戚继光每台只用了50两，验收时上等奖20两银，上上等奖50两银。同年十一月的遵化汤泉大阅兵中，戚继光向阅示大臣汪道昆提出在冲要处再加修200座敌台的请求，经朝廷批准后，第二期工程于万历三年（1575）完工，两期共修敌台1337座，而且越修越好。（昌平镇于嘉靖三十九年因戍守明陵而从蓟镇析出。）

How Much did Qi Jiguang Spend on Building a Watchtower?

In the 6th year of the Longqing reign (1572), the first phase of work supervised by Qi Jiguang was completed, with 1,206 watchtowers built in the Jizhen and Changpingzhen garrisons. If assigned to conscripted workers, it would be difficult to complete a watchtower with 600-1,000 taels of silver. But Qi Jiguang spent only 50 taels on each, in addition to 20 taels for each first-class tower and 50 taels for each superior-class tower. In the Military Parade held at Zunhua hot spring in November of the same year, Qi Jiguang raised a request of building another 200 watchtowers at strategic positions to the inspecting minister Wang Daokun. Upon the approval of the court, the second phase was completed in the 3rd year of the Wanli reign (1575). Altogether 1,337 watchtowers were built in the two phases, with improving quality. (The Changping Garrison was separated from Jizhen Garrison in the 39th year of the Jiajing reign for guarding the Ming mausoleums.)

前杖子长城
The Great Wall at the Qianzhangzi Valley

戚继光足迹遍遵化

隆庆二年（1568）抗倭名将戚继光调任蓟镇后，严武备，整军械，固边关，不仅带出一支训练有素、武器精良、威震敌胆的军队，还使所辖1200多里蓟镇长城变成了城墙高峙、墩台林立、烽堠相望的坚固防线。戚继光"在镇十六年，边备修饬，蓟门宴然"。戍边之余戚继光还扩修了遵化城，加修了汤泉池，创修了永旺塔，鹫峰山、夹山寺、石门峡、冶铁厂到处留下了他的足迹和墨宝。万历十一年（1583）他遭陷离任时，遵化市民罢市，百姓遮首，"辕门遗爱满幽燕，不见胡尘十六年。谁把旌麾移岭表，黄童白叟哭天边"——陈弟诗真实反映了遵化人民对戚继光的拥戴和眷恋。

Qi Jiguang's Footsteps Spread all over Zunhua

In the 2nd year of the Longqing reign (1568), the famous general Qi Jiguang was transferred to Jizhen Garrison. By making strict military preparations, rectifying armament and reinforcing border defense, he not only produced a well-trained army with superior weapons and powerful combat strength but also turned Jizhen section of the Great Wall extending over 1,200 *huali* under his jurisdiction into a solid defense line with lofty walls and numerous watchtowers and beacon towers. "During the 16 years of Qi Jiguang's governance of Jizhen, the border was put in order and the Jimen Pass was at peace." While defending the border, Qi Jiguang also expanded the city of Zunhua, built Tangquan Pool and constructed Yongwang Tower. His footsteps and handwritings are found in many places of Mount Jiufeng, Jiashan Temple, Shimen Gorge and the iron smelter. In the 11th year of the Wanli reign (1583), when Qi Jiguang was forced to leave his post for a false charge, shopkeepers in Zunhua went on strike, and people cried with face covered by hands. "With the benevolent rule of the Yan region by a military genius, no traces of barbarians have been seen for sixteen years. Who issued the order to transfer chief commander's banner to the south of the five ridges? Both the young and the old cried for his absence at the border area."—Chen Di's poem truthfully reflected the respect and love of Zunhua people for Qi Jiguang.

登舍身台

戚继光

向来曾作舍身歌，今日登台意若何？
指点封疆余独感，萧疏鬓发为谁晞。
剑分胡饼从人后，手鞠流泉已自多。
回首朱门歌舞地，尊前列鼎问调和。

断崖垂绠几凭虚，却笑山猿技不如。
古戍春残初见雁，故园愁绝冷看鱼。
百年俯仰谁巾帼，五尺涓埃自简书。
沙碛传餐君莫叹，边臣应得戒衣袽。

A Poem on Sheshen (Self-sacrifice) Platform by Qi Jiguang

While always practicing self-sacrifice
for the benefits of the state,
What feelings will arise during my visit of this platform?
Alone I instructed the reinforcement of the border region,
For whom is my hair becoming sparse and white?
I follow my soldiers to eat hard baked rolls cut with sword,
Well contented with drinking spring water in my hands.
In places where dignitaries abandon themselves to pleasures,
They are enjoying delicacies of every
kind but still grumbling.

My wagon almost dropped from a precipice, But I still laughed,
saying that monkeys could not emulate my skills.
In the ancient garrison,
wild geese are not seen until the end of spring.
In soldiers' hometowns,
their sorrowful wives anxiously await their letters.
Who are heroes in the past century?
I, an insignificant officer,
am stationed here under an imperial order.
Don't sigh over food mixed with sand and stones,
And border officers should live like ascetic monks.

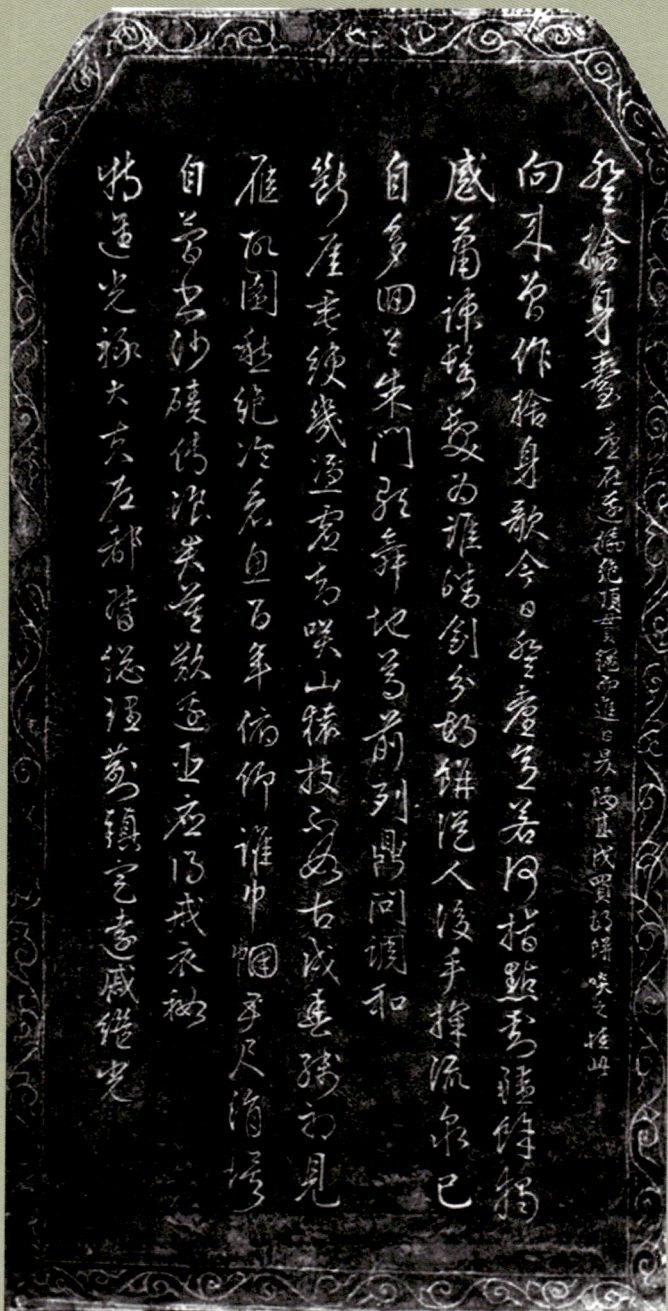

戚继光手书《舍身歌》拓片
Rubbings of Qi Jiguang's calligraphy Poem on Sheshen Platform

戚继光绝唱舍身台

戚继光戎马一生，赤心报国，在抗倭前线写下了"南北驱驰报主情，江花边草笑平生。一年三百六十日，多是横戈马上行"的豪迈诗句。然而，他在北方镇边末期，目睹皇帝昏聩，朝廷无能，官吏腐败，小人弄权，朱门花天酒地与将士"剑分胡饼"、"沙碛传餐"的巨大反差，这位曾叱咤风云的将军登上冀东奇峰舍身台，遥对"尊前列鼎问调和"的京城朱门，愤懑地发出了"萧疏鬓发为谁皤"的质问和呐喊。戚继光挥毫为世人留下千古绝唱《登舍身台》不久，就被发配岭南，后又贬谪回家，一代英豪于万历十五年（1587）在贫困交加中愤然离世。

Qi Jiguang's Poetic Masterpieces Composed on Sheshen Platform

Qi Jiguang spent his entire life fighting for his homeland whole-heartedly, and wrote grand and heroic lines during his resistance against pirate invasions. For example, "I've fought south and north to repay the emperor's benevolence to me, / Flowers and grasses by the river and the border laugh at my plain life. / For three hundred sixty days a year, / I hold my weapon ready atop my steed." However, towards the end of his governance of the northern frontier, he witnessed the great contrast between the imbecility of the emperor, the incompetence of the court, the corruption of officials, the play of politics of base persons, and dignitaries' self-abandonment to pleasures and the enormous hardships endured by generals and soldiers stationed in the border area. This once all-powerful general ascended Sheshen Platform, a great peak in the east of Hebei, angrily threw his question: "for whom is my hair becoming sparse and white" against the remote red gate of the capital city where "they are enjoying delicacies of every kind but still grumbling." Not long after his composition of his poetic masterpiece *Poem on Sheshen Platform*, Qi Jiguang was exiled to the region south of the Five Ridges, and then was forced to retire to his hometown. In the 15th year of the Wanli reign (1587), the hero died in poverty and anger.

戚继光吟诗的舍身台
Sheshen Platform where Qi Jiguang composed his poem

重整残碑缅戚公

2013年，凤凰岭景区的将军台敌台旁，挖出一通残碑，记录了万历十五年（1587）春防期间，蓟辽总督王一鹗、顺天巡抚甕达、监察御史傅光宅等主持修筑饿老婆顶寨敌台的相关情况，很有史料价值。《明史·戚继光传》说："（戚）继光在镇十六年，边备修饬，蓟门晏然。继之者踵其成法，数十年得无事。"将军台的鼎建，阅示碑的树立，对戚继光和他的继任者给予了公正的评价。然而就是这样一位威震敌胆的民族英雄，最后竟死于朝廷排挤和打击。"居正殁半岁，给事中张鼎思言继光不宜于北，当国者遽改之广东。继光悒悒不得志，强一赴，逾年即谢病。给事中张希皋等复劾之，竟罢归。居三年，御史傅光宅疏荐，反夺俸。继光亦遂卒。"也就是说，这通碑竖起的时候，戚继光正好逝去，傅光宅也被夺去了俸禄，都在万历十五年。

❶ 明万历二年（1574），戚继光与朝廷命官为平安城夹山寺题写的匾额拓片
Rubbings of the stele written by Qi Jiguang and other government officials for Jiashan Temple of Ping'an City in the 2nd year of the Wanli reign (1574)

❷ "松棚路题名记"拓片
Rubbing from Stele Record on Naming of Songpenglu Garrison

❸ 修整凤凰岭长城残碑
A residual stele on the restoration of the Great Wall at Fenghuang Ridge

❹ 洪山口明朝古戏楼
An ancient theatre of the Ming dynasty at Hongshan Pass

The Restoration of Stele Relics in Memory of General Qi

In 2013, a residual stele was found from a place near the General's Platform Watchtower of Fenghuang Ridge Scenic Area, which records the related information about the building of the watchtower on Elaopoding Stockaded Village under the supervision of Jiliao Governor Wang Yi'e, Shuntian Grand Coordinator Jian Da, and Investigating Censor Fu Guangzhai, etc. during the period of defense system in the 15th year of the Wanli reign (1587). This stele has great historical value. In *A Biography of Qi Jiguang* of *The History of Ming*, it is written, "During the 16 years of (Qi) Jiguang's governance of the garrison, the border was put in order and the Jimen Pass was at peace. His successors followed his practices and no incident occurred in several decades." The establishment of the General's Platform and the erection of the memorial stele gave a fair comment on Qi Jiguang and his successors. However, this national hero with powerful combat strength that struck terror into the hearts of the enemy died because of the court's exclusion and blow. "Half a year after the death of Zhang Juzheng, an official called *Jishizhong* Zhang Dingsi said that Qi Jiguang was not appropriate for guarding the northern border. And the ruler thus re-assigned him to Guangdong. Qi Jiguang felt frustrated and reluctantly took the office, but retired for sickness the year after. Minister Zhang Xigao impeached him again, and Qi was forced to retire. After three years, Censor Fu Guangzhai rec-ommended him but was deprived of his emolument. Qi Jiguang died not long afterwards." That is to say, when this stele was erected, Qi Jiguang just passed away, and Fu Guangzhai was also deprived of his emolument, both occurring in the 15th year of the Wanli reign.

亦悲亦壮"永熙门"

万历五年（1577）蓟镇总兵戚继光扩修洪山口城竣工后，为城南门镶嵌了一块石质门额，长1.54米，宽0.7米，厚0.19米，刻有"永熙门"三个苍劲大字，以祝边城洪山口永远兴盛安康。时隔52年后的崇祯二年（1629）夏，顺天巡抚王元雅和刚刚上任的蓟镇总兵朱国彦等将官又复修了洪山口城，出于对戚继光爱国精神的景仰和敬佩，他们也将自己的官职和名号刻在了"永熙门"门额左右侧。令人痛惜的是，这年秋天皇太极便率军攻破了洪山口城，继而又拿下了遵化城，在城内的巡抚王元雅见守城无望，上吊自尽。皇太极又回师攻打蓟镇总兵府三屯营，城破之前总兵朱国彦散尽家财，与妻子一起在城墙上面向京师双双自缢身亡。可悲的是，在这之前曾让蓟镇"不见胡尘十六年"的戚继光也因朝廷排挤抑郁贫困而死。这块门额不光映衬着当年征战厮杀的刀光剑影，还记录着一段又一段令人敬佩和扼腕的往事。

The Sublime and Sorrowful Yongxi Gate

In the 5th year of the Wanli reign (1577), after the expansion of the city at Hongshan Pass, the Jizhen Commander-in-Chief Qi Jiguang had a stone tablet inlaid on the southern gate of the city, which was 1.54m long, 0.7m wide and 0.19m thick, inscribed with three big characters "Yong Xi Men", to wish that the border town at Hongshan Pass would be ever prosperous and peaceful. Fifty-two years later in the summer of the 2nd year of the Chongzhen reign (1629), Shuntian Grand Coordinator Wang Yuanya and the new Jizhen Commander-in-Chief Zhu Guoyan as well as other generals repaired the garrison at Hongshan Pass again. Out of their respect and admiration for Qi Jiguang's patriotism, they had their official titles and names inscribed on the left and right sides of the "Yong Xi Men" tablet. Regretfully, in autumn of that year, Huang Taiji led his army to break through Hongshan Pass and then captured Zunhua City. Seeing that it was hopeless to defend the city, Grand Coordinator Wang Yuanya of the city, hanged himself. Huang Taiji returned his troops to attack the Jizhen Commander-in-Chief's office at Santun Garrison. Before the city fell, Commander-in-Chief Zhu Guoyan dispersed all his personal property and hanged himself with his wife on the city wall facing the capital city. Tragically, Qi Jiguang, who once guarded Jizhen Garrison from barbarian invasion for 16 years, had also just died in sorrow and poverty due to the exclusion by the court. This stele not only reflects the shadows of swords in past wars but also records many admirable and regrettable stories.

崇祯三年再修城

崇祯二年（1629）年十月，皇太极率军攻破洪山口驻跸三天又犯遵化，在北京周边饱掠四个月后于崇祯三年（1630）二月退回关外。清军退后，明廷急令修复了被拆毁的洪山口长城。透过这块崇祯三年八月敌台修复碑记，我们似乎还能看到当年两军厮杀和将士急促修城的身影。

Rebuilding the Great Wall in the 3rd Year of Emperor Chongzhen's Reign

In the tenth lunar month of the second year of the reign of Emperor Chongzhen (1629), Huang Taiji led his army to break through the Hongshan Pass and invaded Zunhua after three days' stay there. He did not retreat until the second month of the third year of the reign of Emperor Chongzhen (1630) after four months' plunder in areas around Beijing. After the retreat of the Qing army, the Ming court urgently ordered to repair the destroyed wall at the Hongshan Pass. From the stele record on the repair of the watchtower in the eighth lunar of 1630, we can get a glimpse of the close fight between the two armies and the soldiers' hurried repair of the wall.

❶ 冷嘴头冯良家印有"万历十四年马兰峪造"铭文砖的后院长城
The brick on the Great Wall at Feng Liang's Backyard in the Lengzuitou Pass Village inscribed with "built in the 14th year of the Wanli reign in Malan Valley"

❷ 遵化营天启三年城工碑拓片
Rubbings of a wall work stele made in the 3rd year of Tianqi reign in Zunhua Garrison

❸ 崇祯三年八月洪山口敌台修复碑记
Stele record on the repair of the watchtower in the eighth lunar month of the third year of the reign of Emperor Chongzhen (1630)

平安立碑

盛世修史，平安立碑。自隆庆二年（1568）戚继光开始戍边蓟镇，蓟镇长城十数年安然无事，于是，长城的每个关口、寨堡、敌台、墙体乃至附近的一些城池、庙宇在创修或复修后，都要留下朝廷军政大员的阅示碑或修城记事碑。我市长城一线发现的大量碑刻大都是隆庆、万历年间鼎立的。这些碑刻是长城文化的重要组成部分，是我们了解长城的重要载体，是毁而不复的宝贵财富。

Steles Were Erected in Peacetime

Historical records were compiled in flourishing ages, and steles were erected in peacetime. Since Qi Jiguang started to govern Jizhen Garrison in the 2nd year of the Longqing reign (1568), the Great Wall area in this region was peaceful for over ten years. As a result, steles on inspection by major military officers or on wall building were erected on each pass, stockade, watchtower, wall body and nearby cities and temples along the Great Wall after their establishment or restoration. A large amount of stele inscriptions discovered along the Great Wall of our city were made in the reigns of Longqing and Wanli, which are important parts of the Great Wall culture, important vehicles for our understanding of the Great Wall, and valuable wealth that would never be restored once destroyed.

罗文峪长城万历二年阅示碑拓片
Rubbings of an inspection stele of the 2nd year of the Wanli reign (1574) on the Great Wall at Luowen Valley

大安口长城隆庆四年阅示碑拓片
Rubbings of an inspection stele of the 4th year of the Longqing reign (1570)

官、夫同碑的洪山口万历四十四年《天津春防碑记》碑拓片
Rubbings of the stele on "Spring Defense in Tianjin" of the 44th year of the Wanli reign recording both officers and workers at the Hongshan Pass

巧合得不能再巧合的遵化长城

世上无巧不成书，可世事再巧也没有遵化长城巧得令人不可思议。万里长城东来，爬上洪山口关的苇子岭就进了遵化界，崇山峻岭中留下138华里的伟岸身躯，在最西端的饿老婆顶寨苇子谷（峪）建一雄伟敌台后，便告别遵化蜿蜒西去了（凤凰岭长城《万历三十四年修城记事碑》）。遵化长城的龙头龙尾都腾伏于苍翠碧绿的"苇子"里，你能不称奇叹巧吗！

The Marvelous Coincidence of Zunhua Section of the Great Wall

There is no story without coincidence. But no coincidence is as incredible as the Zunhua section of the Great Wall. The Great Wall which runs from the east enters Zunhua border after it climbs the Weizi Ridge at Hongshan Pass, leaves a stalwart section of 138 *huali* among tall mountains, and winds away from Zunhua westward of a lofty watchtower at Weizi Valley of Elaopoding Stockaded Village at the westernmost end (The Stele on Wall Building in the 34th Year of the Wanli Reign of the Great Wall at Fenghuang Ridge). Both the head and the tail of the dragon-like section of the Great Wall in Zunhua rise and fall among verdant and luxuriant "*weizi*" (reeds). Isn't that a marvelous coincidence?

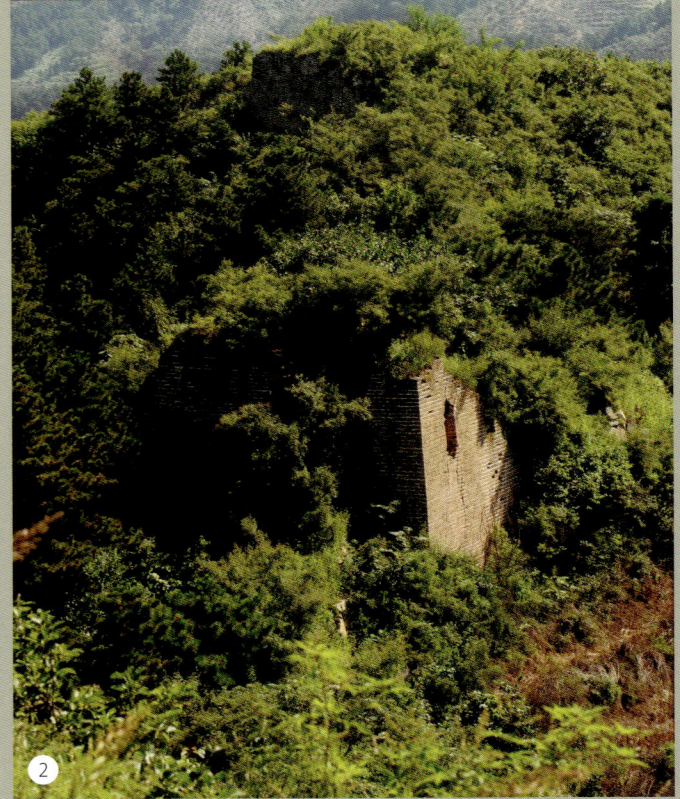

❶ 遵化最东端的
苇子岭长城敌台
The Watchtower at Weizi Ridge
in the easternmost end of Zunhua

❷ 遵化最西端的
苇子谷（峪）长城敌台遗址
Ruins of the Watchtower at Weizi Valley
at the westernmost end of Zunhua

最早和最晚的遵化明长城建筑

据已发现的修城石刻和志载，遵化明石长城最早大规模修筑时间为嘉靖三十年（1551），这以后连年不断的大修筑工程，才把断断续续的万里明长城连为一体，隆庆三年（1569）后又在石墙的基础上修筑了敌台和包砖墙。石刻记载洪山口城北楼创修、罗文峪关下营重修都在崇祯十年（1637），再过七年大明王朝就覆亡了，这是遵化已发现的有碑记载最晚的长城建筑。

The Earliest and the Latest Structures of Zunhua Section of the Ming Great Wall

Based on the available stone inscriptions and historical records on the construction of the Great Wall, the earliest large-scale construction of the Ming stone Great Wall in Zunhua occurred in the 30th year of the Jiajing reign (1551), and the intermittent sections of the Ming Great Wall were not integrated until constant large-scale construction work in the following years were completed. After the 3rd year of the Longqing reign (1569), watchtowers and brick-covered walls were built on the basis of stone walls. According to the records on stone inscriptions, both the establishment of Northern Tower at Hongshan Pass and the reconstruction of Guanxia Garrison at the Luowen Valley occurred in the 10th year of the Chongzhen reign (1637), seven years before the Ming dynasty was overthrown. These are the latest Great Wall structures recorded on stele discovered in Zunhua.

崇祯十年创修的洪山口北楼
The Northern Tower at Hongshan Pass built in the 10th year of the Chongzhen reign (1637)

① 铭文：罗文谷军夫修完迤东边城三十七丈
Inscription: Military workers of Luowen Valley completed 37 *zhang* of the border wall extending eastward

② 铭文：忠义中卫迤西雇募夫修完工程一十一丈
Inscription: Zhongyi Middle Wei employed conscripted workers to complete 11 *zhang* of the wall extending westward

③ 铭文：忠义中卫迤东雇募夫大修完工程一十一丈
Inscription: Zhongyi Middle Wei employed conscripted workers to overhaul 11 *zhang* of the wall extending eastward

④ 铭文：丰润县东界
Inscription: The eastern boundary of Fengrun County

⑤ 铭文：界 将军石迤西修完边城三十五丈
Inscription: Boundary   35 *zhang* of the border wall was completed west of the General Stone

⑥ 铭文：修完第三工十四丈起派夫
Inscription: Workers were dispatched after the third phase (14 *zhang*) was completed

⑦ 铭文：兴州前屯卫以东分修三十五丈 嘉靖三十一年四月初二日完
Inscription: 35 *zhang* was completed east of the Qiantun Wei of the Xingzhou Prefecture on the 2nd day of the 4th lunar month, the 31st year of the Jiajing reign (1552)

⑧ 铭文：雇募修忠义中卫迤东修完边城一十三丈
Inscription: Workers were employed to completed 13 *zhang* of the border wall east of Zhongyi Middle Wei

刻在巨石上的修城活档案

在遵化长城上，我们发现了18块刻字的修墙界石，它为世人提供了丰富而确凿的修城信息。一是修城年代，如"三十一年四月二日完（1552）""嘉靖三十二年四月（1553）"；二是修城人工来源，如"军夫修完边墙三十七丈""雇募夫修完工程一十一丈"；三是修城分包机构，地方包修的有：遵化城、玉田、丰润；军队包修的有：遵化卫（驻遵化）、忠义中卫（驻遵化）、兴州前屯卫（驻丰润）、镇朔卫（驻蓟州）、罗文谷军夫等；四是修城工程量。这些巨大的修墙界石浸满了募夫、军夫的血泪和汗水，是他们为我们中华民族修筑了一条震撼世界、彪炳千秋的万里长城。壮哉，遵化有部刻在巨石上的修城活档案！

Living Archives on Wall Building Inscribed on Huge Rocks

On Zunhua section of the Great Wall, we discovered 18 boundary stones with inscriptions about wall building, which offer rich and accurate information on wall building to the world as follows: first, the time of wall building, for example, "completed on the second day of the fourth lunar month, the 31st year (1552)", "the fourth lunar month, the 32nd year of the Jiajing reign (1553)". Second, the sources of laborers for building the wall, for example, "37 *zhang* of the border wall was completed by military workers", and "workers were employed to complete 11 *zhang* of the work". Third, subcontracting agencies for wall building, with local subcontractors including Zunhua town, Yutian, and Fengrun, and military subcontractors including Zunhua Wei (stationed in Zunhua), Zhongyi Middle Wei (stationed in Zunhua), Qiantun Wei of Xingzhou (stationed in Fengrun), Zhenshuo Wei (stationed in Ji Prefecture), military workers of Luowen Valley, among others. Fourth, the amount of work done for building the wall. These huge boundary stones about wall building are representations of the blood, tears and sweat of conscripted workers and military workers, who built the world-famous Great Wall shining through the ages. Alas, Zunhua has a living archive on wall building inscribed on huge rocks!

⑨ 铭文：分界 遵化城保修完迤西边城一十五丈

Inscription: Boundary　Zunhua town guards completed 15 *zhang* of the wall extending eastward

⑩ 铭文：1.忠义中卫迤东修完工程一十三丈起　2.兴州前屯卫迤西修完工一丈四尺起派夫修

Inscription: 1. Starting from the 13 *zhang* of the work completed east of Zhongyi Middle Wei　2. The 1.4 *zhang* in the west was completed by people sent by Qiantun Wei of Xingzhou Prefecture

⑪ 铭文：界 玉田□□完□迤西五丈

Inscription: Boundary　Yutian Completed　5 *zhang* westward

⑫ 铭文：忠义中卫迤西修完边城一十五丈雇募修

Inscription: Zhongyi Middle Wei had 15 *zhang* of the westward border wall completed by employed workers

⑬ 铭文：镇朔卫

Inscription: Zhenshuo Wei

⑭ 铭文：界碑

Inscription: Boundary Stele

⑮ 铭文：石 界石

Inscription: Stone　Boundary Stone

⑯ 铭文：雇募迤东边城一十二丈

Inscription: 12 *zhang* of the border wall eastward was completed by employed workers

⑰ 铭文：分界 黄崖口迤东修完边城三十五丈 嘉靖三十二年四月

Inscription: Boundary　35 *zhang* of the border wall was completed east of the Huangya Pass　The fourth lunar month of the 32nd year of Jiajing reign

⑱ 铭文：界 遵化卫迤西一十二丈五尺雇募夫修

Inscription: Boundary　12.5 *zhang* of the border wall west of Zunhua Wei was completed by employed workers

九关鱼钥控雄图

"大道为关，小道为口。屯军为营，猎守为寨。"蓟镇为万里长城九军镇中最重要一镇，设十二路，遵化占两路，辖六营，辟九关，扎二十二寨。

两路：松棚路（后由松棚营改为洪山口）、马兰路（马兰峪）；六营：松棚营（洪山口）、罗文峪营（北下营）、沙坡峪营（曹家堡）、大安口营（西下营）、鲇鱼石营（鲇鱼池）、马兰营（马兰峪）；九关：由东向西依次为洪山口关、马蹄峪关、罗文峪关、沙坡峪关、冷嘴头关、大安口关、鲇鱼石关、马兰谷关、宽佃峪关。

Nine Passes Command Strategic Positions Like a Fish-Shaped Key

"A big pass is called *guan*, while a small pass is called *kou*. Towns that are stationed with troops are called *ying*, and villages stockaded are called *zhai*." Jizhen was the most important of the nine garrisons along the Great wall, which had 12 *lu* garrisons, two of which were in Zunhua, six *ying*, nine passes and 22 stockaded villages.

Two *lu* garrisons: Songpenglu (later changed to the Hongshan Pass), and Malanlu (Malan Valley); six *ying* garrisons: Songpeng (Hongshan Pass), Luowenyu (Beixia Garrison), Shapoyu (Caojia Fort), Da'ankou (Xi'xia Garrison), Nianyushi (Nianyu Pond), Malan (Malan Valley); nine passes: Hongshan, Matiyu, Luowenyu, Shapoyu, Lengzhuitou, Da'ankou, Nianyushi, Malangu, and Kuandianyu from east to west respectively.

琵琶峪长城
The Great Wall at Pipa Valley

军事重镇遵化

洪武十一年（1378）因遵化控扼塞外通往北平的贡路（今邦宽路）和罗文峪进关要道，始置遵化卫（隶属北平都司）。永乐初，成祖弃大宁卫给兀良哈，徙东胜右卫于遵化（隶属后军都督府）。为加强长城防守，永乐元年遵化又增置了忠义中卫（隶属后军都督府），徙置了宽河守御千户所（隶属大宁都司），戚继光镇边时又增置了左营、右营和辎重营。顺天巡抚、都察院公署、总镇行署、监视行署、遵化道署、游击署、运饷通判署、督饷厅、守备府公署等行政和军事机关也都设于遵化。随着军事作用不断增强，遵化城修得更加坚固壮观，时有"铜遵化，铁卢龙，秸秆儿插的玉田城"之说。

遵化古城北门
North gate of the ancient
city of Zunhua

遵化古城西门
West gate of the ancient
city of Zunhua

Zunhua as a Strategic Military City

In the 11th year of the Hongwu reign (1378), Zunhua Wei Garrison (under the jurisdiction of the Beiping Dusi, or Beiping Regional Military Commission) was established as Zunhua controlled the tributary road from outside the Great Wall to Beiping (present-day Bangkuan Road) and a strategic pass to Luowen Valley. In the early years of the Yongle reign, Emperor Chengzu surrendered Daning Wei Garrison to Uriankhai, and moved the Dongsheng Right Wei Garrison to Zunhua (under the jurisdiction of the Back Military Commission). To strengthen the defense at the Great Wall, in the first year of the Yongle reign, Zhongyi Middle Wei Garrison was added to Zunhua (under the jurisdiction of the Back Military Commission), and the Kuanhe Thousand Household Bureau of Defense was moved here (under the jurisdiction of the Daning Military Department). During Qi Jiguang's governance of the border town, the Left Garrison, the Right Garrison and Zizhong Garrison were added. There also established a couple of administrative and military departments such as Shuntian Grand Coordinator, office of the Department of Supervision, administrative office of Commander-in-Chief, administrative office of Surveillance, office of Zunhua Daoyuan Official, Office of Guerrilla Warfare, Office of Pay Transportation Magistrate, Department of Pay Supervision, and office of Garrison Officer, etc. With the constant strengthening of its military functions, the city of Zunhua was increasingly reinforced, appearing more and more spectacular. There was a saying of "bronze Zunhua, iron Lulong and Yutian city built by straws" during that time.

万历九年（1581）戚继光重修遵化城北城门门额"拱极门"
"Gongjimen" on the architrave of the north gate of the ancient city of Zunhua rebuilt b
Qi Jiguang in the 9th year of Wanli reign (1581)

蓟镇（遵化长城）兵制系统示意图

Diagram of the military defense system of Jizhen Garrison (Zunhua section of the Great Wall)

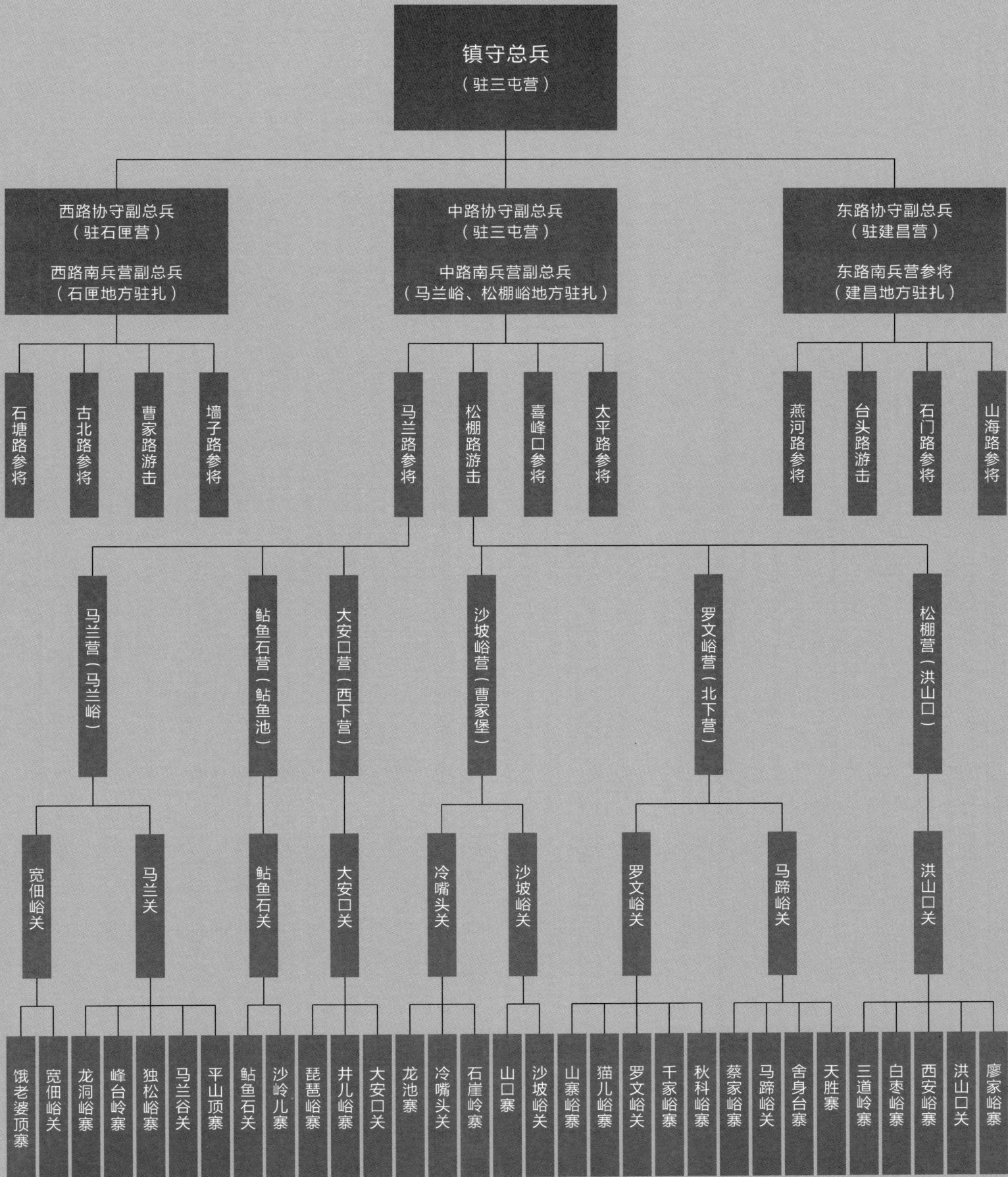

镇守总兵
（驻三屯营）

西路协守副总兵
（驻石匣营）
西路南兵营副总兵
（石匣地方驻扎）

中路协守副总兵
（驻三屯营）
中路南兵营副总兵
（马兰峪、松棚峪地方驻扎）

东路协守副总兵
（驻建昌营）
东路南兵营参将
（建昌地方驻扎）

石塘路参将   古北路参将   曹家路游击   墙子路参将

马兰路参将   松棚路游击   喜峰口参将   太平路参将

燕河路参将   台头路游击   石门路参将   山海路参将

马兰营（马兰峪）   鲇鱼石营（鲇鱼池）   大安口营（西下营）   沙坡峪营（曹家堡）   罗文峪营（北下营）   松棚营（洪山口）

宽佃峪关   马兰关   鲇鱼石关   大安口关   冷嘴头关   沙坡峪关   罗文峪关   马蹄峪关   洪山口关

饿老婆顶寨   宽佃峪关   龙洞峪寨   峰台岭寨   独松峪寨   马兰谷关   平山顶寨   鲇鱼石关   沙岭儿寨   琵琶峪寨   井儿峪寨   大安口关   龙池寨   冷嘴头关   石崖岭寨   山口寨   沙坡峪关   山寨峪寨   猫儿峪寨   罗文峪关   千家峪寨   秋科峪寨   蔡家峪寨   马蹄峪关   舍身台寨   天胜寨   三道岭寨   白枣峪寨   西安峪寨   洪山口关   廖家峪寨

参照 明《四镇三关志》

Reference: *The Annals on Four Garrisons and Three Passes* of the Ming dynasty

逶迤东来 奔腾壮阔——
第一关：洪山口关

遵化城东北42华里的小厂乡境内洪山口关，是遵化长城最东端的一道雄关。关城明洪武年间建，弘治年间改为松棚营城。几经扩建后，营城东西长400米，南北宽200米，驻军227员，军械310件，先是游击后改参将镇守。传唐朝洪姓人家在此守关，故名洪山口。洪山口关极冲，皇太极曾破此关占遵化犯北京，又是冀东八路军的诞生地和成长摇篮。城内现存明代戏楼因掩护过抗日名将包森而被百姓尊崇为"福楼"。

全长20华里的洪山口长城，设廖家峪寨、洪山口关、西安峪寨、白枣峪寨、三道岭寨和松棚路城，是我市境内保存较好的长城。遵化长城有246座敌台，现存较完整的只剩18座，而洪山口竟幸存6座，完整的砖长城也是全市最长的。这里还有"品"字形古路城、千总洼、官道沟、园楼沟、营房沟、小官岭、横跨墙体里外通透的砖拱通道和真武阁遗址，是遵化明长城的博物馆。

A Gigantic Dragon
Galloping from the East
The First Pass: Hongshan Pass

The Hongshan Pass within Xiaochang Township 42 *huali* northeast of Zunhua is the easternmost pass of Zunhua section of the Great Wall. The pass was built in the Hongwu reign of the Ming dynasty and renamed Songpenglu Garrison in the Hongzhi reign. After several expansions, the garrison extended 400m from east to west, 200m from north to south, and used to be guarded by 227 soldiers with 310 weapons. It was first used for guerrilla warfare and later governed by *canjiang* (lit. "staff general"). It was so named because a family named Hong once settled here to guard the place. The Hongshan Pass occupies a strategic position. Huang Taiji once broke through this pass to occupy Zunhua and then invade Beijing. It was also a birthplace and a cradle for the Eighth Route Army of east Hebei. A Ming theatrical stage of the Ming dynasty extant in the town is respectfully called Tower of Blessing by the local people because it once protected Bao Sen, a famous general in the War of Resistance against Japanese Aggression.

The Hongshankou section of the Great Wall is 20 *huali* long, which covers Liaojiayu Stockaded Village, Hongshan Pass, Xi'anyu Stockaded Village, Baizaoyu Stockaded Village, Sandaoling Stockaded Village, and Songpenglu Garrison, and is a section that has been well preserved in Zunhua. Zunhua section of the Great Wall has 246 watchtowers, of which only 18 are intact including 6 at Hongshan Pass. The complete brick Great Wall extant at the Pass is also the longest in the whole city. Hongshan Pass is like a museum of the Ming Great Wall in Zunhua, with a delta-shaped ancient town, Qianzong Marsh Land, Guandao Trench, Yuanlou Trench, Yingfang Trench, Xiaoguan Ridge, transparent brick-arch passage across the wall, and ruins of Zhenwu Pavilion.

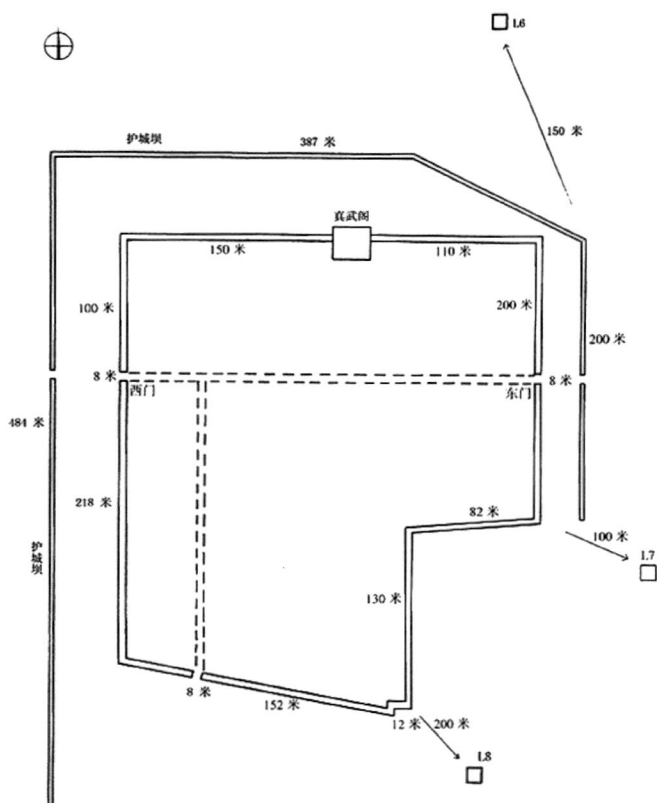

洪山口路城平面图（河北文研所测绘）
The floor plan of Hongshan Pass (drawn by Hebei Cultural Institute)

洪山口长城
The Great Wall at Hongshan Pass

白枣峪长城

The Great Wall at Baizao Valley

修建于明崇祯年间的洪山口护楼北楼
The northern tower of a Protective Tower at Hongshan Pass built in the reign of Chongzhen in the Ming dynasty

洪山口护楼

崇祯年间，皇太极率军破洪山口犯遵化逼北京后，朝廷重新补修加固了洪山口一线长城和作为松棚路路城的洪山口城，在城东、南、北增建了"护楼"。现东楼、南楼遗迹还在，北楼完好。近四百来年，它像一位站在高高山岗上的勇士，风餐露宿，忠诚地护佑着洪山口。勤劳的洪山口人也未冷落这位好心的"哨兵"，每逢除夕，男女老少就成群结队来鸣炮上香，顶礼膜拜，把个北楼当作神物一样来祭祀。

Guard Towers at Hongshan Pass

During the Chongzhen reign, following Huang Taiji's breakthrough into Hongshan Pass to occupy Zunhua and invade Beijing, the court repaired and reinforced the frontier Great Wall at Hongshan Pass and the city of Hongshan Pass which served as Songpenglu Garrison, adding guard towers in its east, south and north. Now the ruins of the eastern and southern towers are still there, while the northern tower is preserved intact, which has been loyally guarding Hongshan Pass like a loyal warrior on the tall mountain for nearly 400 years. Diligent people of Hongshan Pass think highly of this kind-hearted guard. On every New Year's Eve, local people pay homage to the northern tower with fireworks and burning incense.

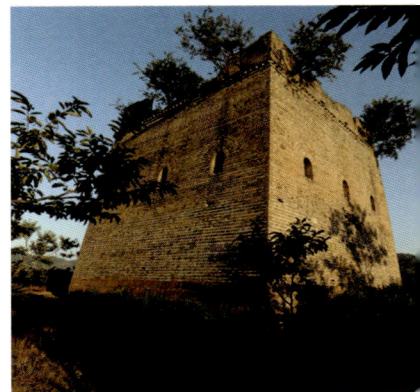

修建于明崇祯年间的洪山口护楼北楼
The northern guard tower at Hongshan Pass built in the reign of Chongzhen in the Ming dynasty

The Great Wall at Xiaoguan Ridge

The Great Wall at Xiaoguan Ridge is a tiger-skin-colored stone wall, while the section next to it is a brick-covered wall. There is a local saying that a petty officer, who presided over the construction, built a stone wall instead of a brick one to reduce materials and embezzle money. Qi Jiguang, enraged at the corruptive act, had the petty officer killed by huge nails and buried on a ridge inside the border wall as a punishment for him. Hence the name of Xiaoguan (lit. "petty officer") Ridge and Xiaoguan Tomb. After the establishment of the People's Republic of China, local Party organizations frequently mentioned the story of the petty officer to indicate that cadres should work hard for the people and be clean and honest in their governance. In the 1960s, a farmer surnamed Zhang led a team to seek treasures by digging into the tomb, only to find a skeleton and two huge nails. In fact, there were strict rules for the building of the Great Wall in the Ming dynasty. How came that a petty officer was allowed to corrupt as he liked on such a large project? Why was he killed? No historical record has been found on this story, and perhaps only the floating rosy cloud over the ridge knows what really happened.

小官今何在，彩云空悠悠

小官岭长城为虎皮石墙，而临界便是砖包墙，百姓说是带工的小官偷工减料，贪占银两，把砖墙修成了石墙。戚继光查验时对这种欺骗朝廷的贪腐行为十分震怒，用巨钉穿骨处死小官并葬关墙里侧山岭上罚他永世守边，这便有了"小官岭"和"小官坟"。解放后，地方党组织时常拿惩处小官的故事告诫干部要勤政为民，廉洁自守。上世纪六十年代一张姓农民带人掘坟找宝，只寻得一具骷髅，两根巨钉。其实，明长城的修筑是有严格规制的，偌大个一号工程哪容得了一个带工小官恣意妄为呢！小官何以被杀？只听传说，没见志载，个中缘由或许只有悠悠彩云才晓得。

遵化人始创三屯营

明景泰四年（1453），蓟镇第六任总兵宗胜始派驻遵化忠义中卫的高名、程兴、史允三个百户长到县域东大王庄屯田戍边，因遵化的三个百户长率三百军户在这里屯田，故称大王庄为三屯营。天顺二年（1458），蓟镇第七任总兵胡镛将蓟镇治所从峥子峪移至三屯营，从而开启了三屯营186年的镇治基业。

万历四年（1576），戚继光扩建三屯营竣工后，蓟辽总督杨兆见新城雄伟高大，督府殿宇轩昂，镇湖清波旖旎，欣然赋诗——"金城百二支祈伏，虎观云流第一枢。千里鸡斯归匹练，九关鱼钥控雄图。浮空日月重闉绕，入望山河列雉扶。汉册从来知定远，又看碣石颂平胡"，并书丹，勒石成碑，立于镇府。旧时，常有墨客拓碑留宝，民国时国军士兵穷急，也常拓碑卖到京城。

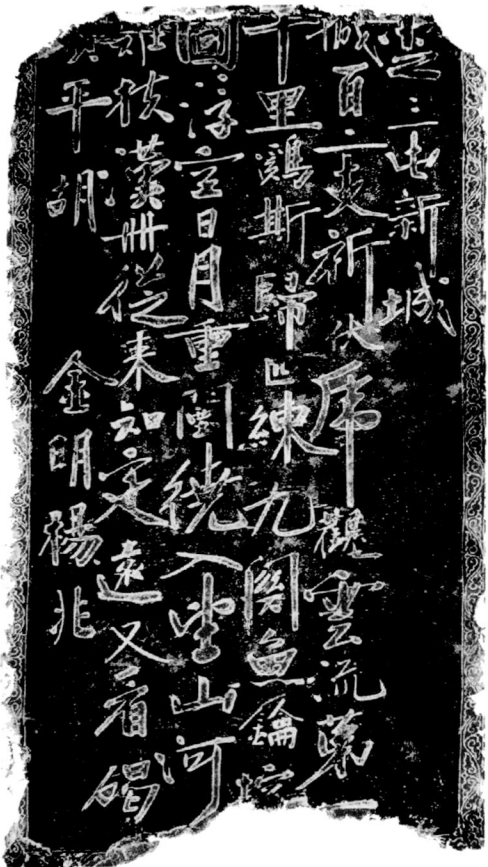

蓟辽总督杨兆
三屯新城题诗碑拓片
Rubbings of the stele of the poem composed by
Jiliao Governor Yang Zhao on the new garrison of Santun Garrison

The Santun Garrison Invented by Zunhua Residents

In the 4th year of the Jingtai reign (1453) in the Ming dynasty, Zong Sheng, the sixth Commander-in-Chief of Jizhen Garrison, dispatched Gao Ming, Cheng Xing and Shi Yun, three leaders of hundred households stationed in Zhongyi Middle *Wei* Unit of Zunhua, to Dawang Village east of the county seat to reclaim wasteland and guard the frontier. Dawang Village was thus called Santun Garrison. In the 2nd year of Tianshun reign (1458), the seventh Commander-in-Chief of Jizhen Garrison, Hu Yong, removed the headquarters of the garrison from Zhizi Valley to Santun Garrison, thus starting the governance of Santun Garrison lasting for 186 years.

In the 4th year of the Wanli reign (1576), following the expansion of Santun Garrison by Qi Jiguang, Yang Zhao, the Governor of Ji and Liao, was in the right mood to compose a poem at the sight of the lofty new garrison with a magnificent office building and a rippling garrison lake. The poem reads, "The impregnable city stands lofty,/As the first invincible hub with crouching tigers and floating clouds./Soldiers returned from their drills in early morning,/and the nine passes command strategic positions like a fish-shaped key./Attended by the sun and the moon high above in the sky,/The city watches the mountains and rivers to guard the state./Since the Han dynasty we've been defending our remote borders,/And now we eulogize again for the pacification of barbarian tribes." The poem was written in red ink and inscribed on a stele, which was erected on the town seat. In the past, literary men often had rubbings from the stele as their treasure. In the Republic of China, poor soldiers often sold rubbings of the stele to Beijing.

官道沟

这个狭长的山谷叫官道沟，是弘治十二年（1499）都御史洪钟将松棚营营城改到洪山口后开辟的一条通往镇城三屯营的交通通道，将士、兵器、军粮都从这里往来运输。

Guandao Trench

This narrow and long valley called Guandao Trench was a traffic corridor opened by Censor Hong Zhong in the 12th year of Hongzhi reign by moving Songpeng Garrison to Hongshan Pass, via which soldiers, weapons and grains were transported.

关山跌宕　雄峻险奇——
第二关：马蹄峪关

遵化城北偏东23华里的侯家寨乡境内马蹄峪关，是遵化长城东数第二道雄关，设天胜、舍身台、马蹄峪、蔡家峪四关寨，完整敌台六座。关城洪武年间依山而建，周长600米，城高4.5米，辟东、南两门，街呈十字，城内有泉，泉边有寺，寺中有僧，城北建有一座6米高台，台上设有真武阁。关城驻千总一人，军卒102人。登高远望，不规则的关城酷似马蹄，故将此关称为马蹄峪。

A Horse's Hoof among the Undulating Steep Mountains—the Second Pass: Matiyu Pass

Matiyu Pass in Houjiazhai Township 23 *huali* northeast of Zunhua is the second pass from the east on Zunhua section of the Great Wall, on which there are four stockades, namely, Tiansheng, Sheshen Platform, Mati Valley and Caijia Valley, and six integral watchtowers. The pass was built along the mountains in the Hongwu reign, which was 4.5m high with a perimeter of 600m, having eastern and southern gates. The streets took a cross shape. There was a spring in the town, by which there was a temple, with monks there. In the north of the town, there was a six-meter platform, on which there was Zhenwu Pavilion. The pass used to be guarded by a brigade commander leading 102 soldiers. Seen from afar on a tall mountain, the irregular pass looks like a horse's hoof, and is therefore named Matiyu Pass (Mati means horse's hoof).

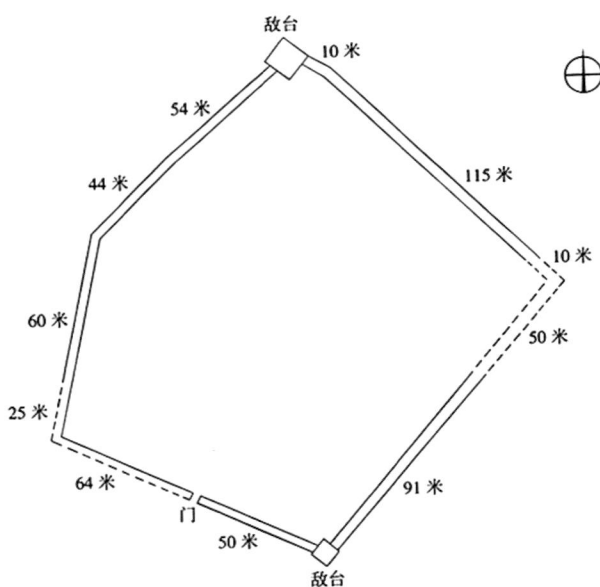

马蹄峪关城平面图（河北文研所测绘）
The floor plan of Matiyu Pass (drawn by Hebei Cultural Institute)

舍身台长城
The Great Wall at Sheshen Platform

马蹄峪长城
The Great Wall at Mati Valley

跌宕起伏的马蹄峪长城

马蹄峪长城，横跨海拔745米的黑锅顶及鹫峰山等群峰，跌宕起伏，攀腾跳跃，远望其势，犹如绿海跃起的蛟龙，蔚为壮观。六座完整敌台中，有的占势突兀，有的门楣精美，有的巨石厮守，有的相望落差巨大。因山势雄险，马蹄峪口东不仅全为四等虎皮石墙，还留存了许多北齐长城。马蹄峪关至河口边墙走势艰险，难以攀爬，是探险家和驴友的乐园。马蹄峪口西山势趋缓，除有一段砖包墙外，其余为虎皮石墙。

The Undulating Great Wall at Mati Valley

The Great Wall at Mati Valley is like a spectacular dragon soaring up from a green sea and undulating over peaks such as the 745m-high Heiguo Peak and Mount Jiufeng. Of the six complete watchtowers extant, some are on towering positions, some have exquisite architecture, some are guarded by huge rocks, and some have a great gap in elevation. Due to its precipitousness, the walls east of Matiyu Pass are all fourth-class tiger-skin-colored stone walls, and many sections of the Northern Qi Great Wall have been well preserved. The section from Matiyu Pass to Hekou Border Wall, which is so steep and perilous that it is very difficult to climb, offers a wonderland for explorers and hikers. The mountain slope becomes gentler west of Matiyu Pass, and the wall consists of tiger-skin-colored stone sections except for one brick-covered stone section.

马蹄峪长城
The Great Wall at Mati Valley

右图：舍身台长城
The picture on the right: The Great Wall at Sheshen Platform

长城寻宝人
Treasure hunters on the Great Wall

深山老峪找"金墩"

传马蹄峪关东山尖和山洼分别由两位把总带工各建一敌楼，尖楼把总粗工滥造，基石不整，砖瓦不齐，草草修完报功，验收官远望山尖敌台耸立好不气派，便奏请朝廷封官加赏；而洼楼把总精工细作，齐整整条石垒了十一层，砖角齐整，勾抹平实，石拱门上还刻了精致砖雕，朝廷治罪把这个延工的把总杀了。戚继光查阅边关才得昭雪，奏朝廷给误杀的把总铸金头重葬，百姓们称之为"金墩"。多少辈子不知有多少人寻遍深山老峪终不得"金墩"，忽一日一白叟空中道："无需找，只要尔等本分做人，凭心做事，家中自会有黄金墩。"

Seeking the "Gold Mound" among Remote Mountains

It is said that two squad leaders were assigned to build a watchtower on the peak and valley of the eastern mountain of Matiyu Pass respectively. The officer in charge of the peak tower roughly finished the project, with uneven corner-stones, bricks and tiles, and reported his work early. The watchtower on the peak looked very stately when viewed from afar, so that the inspector asked the court to promote and reward the officer. But the officer in charge of the valley tower worked very meticulously, laid 11 layers with even strip stones, lined bricks neatly and solidly, and even had exquisite brick sculpture made on a stone arch gate. But as his work was delayed, the latter officer was killed by the court, a mistake not redressed until Qi Jiguang inspected the border. Qi requested that the officer killed by mistake be reburied with his head encased with gold. The officer's tomb is called the Gold Mound by the local people. Numerous people have searched the remote mountains and valleys for the Gold Mound in vain. A white-haired old man became enlightened one day, "You don't need to look for it any more. So long as you behave yourselves and work honestly, a gold mound will arise at your own home."

❶　做工粗糙的马蹄峪尖楼
The roughly built tower on the peak of Mati Valley

❷　敌台精品——马蹄峪洼子楼
A watchtower masterpiece—Tower at Mati Valley

❸　马蹄峪关东侧北齐长城
The Northern Qi Great Wall east of Matiyu Pass

塞北锁钥 震古烁今——
第三关：罗文峪关

遵化城北20华里的侯家寨乡境内罗文峪关，是遵化长城东数第三道雄关，洪武十四年（1381）重建，传当年隋朝建关时由一位叫罗文的将军镇守而得名，设秋科峪、甘查峪（干家峪）、罗文峪、猫儿峪、山寨峪和罗文峪营（北下营），完整敌台四座。此关北通大川，南守古城，战略位置极为冲要，驻军304人，马六匹，军械320件，它和喜峰口关发生过著名的长城抗战。

A Strategic Pass on the North Border Celebrated Throughout the Ages— The Third Pass: Luowenyu Pass

Luowenyu Pass in the Houjiazhai Township 20 *huali* north of Zunhua is the third lofty pass from the east on Zunhua section of the Great Wall, which was rebuilt in the 14th year of the Hongwu reign (1381), and got its name from the legend that a general called Luo Wen was once stationed there when the pass was built in the Sui dynasty. The pass has the Qiuke Valley, Gancha Valley (the Ganjia Valley), the Luowen Valley, the Mao'er Valley, the Shanzhai Valley and the Luowenyu Garrison (Beixia Garrison), and four complete watchtowers. This pass occupies a very strategic position as it leads to a big river in the north and protects the ancient city in the south. The pass used to be guarded by 304 soldiers with six horses and 320 weapons. Famous battles against Japanese invaders were fought on this pass and the Xifeng Pass.

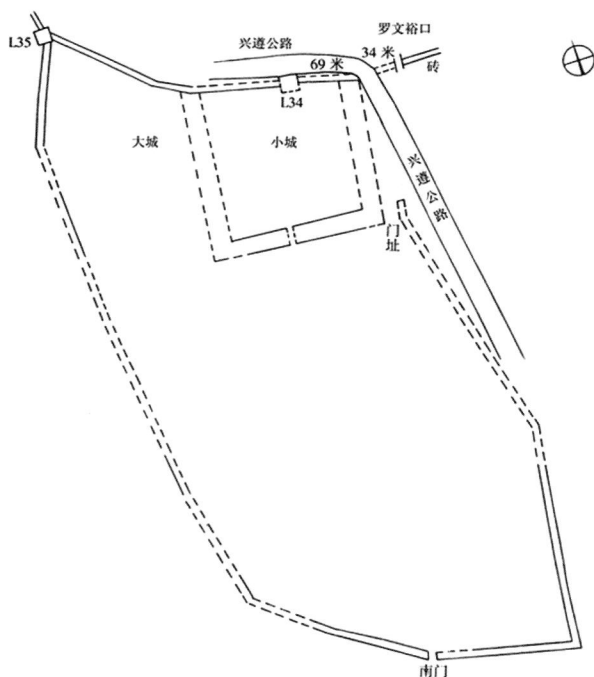

罗文峪关城平面图（河北文研所测绘）
The floor plan of Luowenyu Pass (drawn by Hebei Cultural Institute)

后杖子长城

The Great Wall at Houzhangzi Village

罗文峪长城
The Great Wall at Luowen Valley

后杖子长城
The Great Wall at Houzhangzi Village

左图：
所谓"一步越千年"
的后杖子明长城砖石垛口

The picture on the left page:
A brick-stone crenel on the Ming
Great Wall at Houzhangzi from
which one can traverse 1,000
years in one step according to legend

"嘉靖"石头"万历"砖
何来一步越千年

嘉靖十八年（1539）前长城还是"碎石干磊，遇水则冲，虏
过即平，其何以守"（都御史戴金语）互不连接的简单阻隔
之墙。震动朝野的"庚戌事变"后，遵化境内从嘉靖三十年
（1551）开始横贯东西大规模修筑石长城，特别是经戚继光
十几年修筑，才有了246座敌台和双面砖包、单面砖包、砖
石混合边墙。在后杖子长城砖石垛口交汇处，不免让人陡生
"一步越千年"（北齐至明朝）的冥思遐想。驻足细看，这
段长城一边是嘉靖年间的虎皮石垛口、石马道（四等墙），一
边是万历年间的砖垛口、石马道（三等墙），哪儿有北齐长
城的影子？其实这一步只迈过了短命的隆庆朝（六年），何来
"一步越千年"！1982年省文研所在后杖子明长城勘测报告中
写道："此段墙体分为三段，中间砖砌，两端用毛石白灰砌
成。"（《明蓟镇长城》卷七）

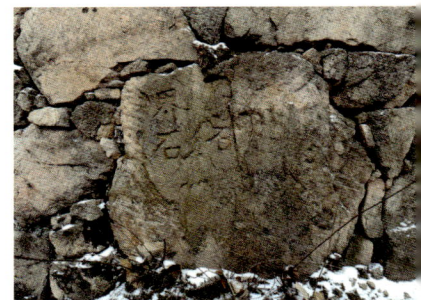

后杖子长城东侧修墙界石
Boundary stone about wall
building east of the Great Wall at
Houzhangzi Village

With Jiajing-period Stones and Wanli-period Bricks, How Can One Traverse 1,000 Years in One Step

Before the 18th year of the Jiajing reign (1539), the Great Wall consisted of merely disconnected walls for simple blocking, which were built with gravels. It could be easily washed away by water, and flattened when invaders crossed, not strong enough to defend the state (words of Censor Dai Jin). After the Gengxu War startling both the court and commonalty, large-scale stone walls were built from east to west in Zunhua starting from the 30th year of the Jiajing reign (1551). In particular, with Qi Jiguang's work in over one decade, 246 watchtowers and border walls with double brick cover, single brick cover and brick-stone mixture appeared. At the convergence of the walls of Houzhangzi Great Wall, people tend to think that they traverse 1,000 years with one step (from the Northern Qi dynasty to the Ming dynasty). But a careful scrutiny of the walls will discover that one side of the wall consists of tiger-skin-colored stone crenels and stone riding track (fourth-grade wall) of the Jiajing reign, while the other side of the wall consists of the brick crenels and stone riding track of the Wanli reign (third-grade wall), having not the slightest trace of the Northern Qi Great Wall. In fact, this step only traverses the short-lived Longqing reign (6 years) instead of 1,000 years! The report of Hebei Cultural Institute on the survey of the Ming Great Wall at Houzhangzi in 1982 reads, "This wall has three sections, with the middle section built with bricks and the two ends with stone blocks and lime." (*The Ming Great Wall in Jizhen Garrison*, Vol. 7)

墩堠相望　古韵犹存——
第四关：沙坡峪关

遵化城北偏西22华里的兴旺寨乡境内沙坡峪关是遵化长城东数第四道雄关，也是松棚路所辖最西的一道关口，洪武十四年（1381）建，设山口寨、沙坡峪关和沙坡峪营（曹家堡），完整敌台一座。沙坡峪关城周长540米，内有城隍庙，驻军148人，兵器80件，马一匹。城南有一座三亩大公园，18个石阶直通关城。沙坡峪初叫三坡峪，后因村南土质为沙，而改称沙坡峪。

A Gallery of Historical Sites in Zunhua— the Fourth Pass: Shapoyu Pass

The Shapoyu Pass in the Xingwangzhai Township 22 *huali* northwest of Zunhua city is the fourth impregnable pass on Zunhua section of the Great Wall, and is also the westernmost pass governed by Songpenglu Garrison. Established in the 14th year of the Hongwu reign (1381), the pass has Shankou Stockaded Village, Shapoyu Pass and the Shapoyu Garrison (present-day Caojiabao), as well as a complete watchtower. The Pass, with a perimeter of 540m, had a town god's temple, and used to be guarded by 148 soldiers with 80 weapons and one horse. In the south of the town was a big park covering an area of 3 mu (1 mu = 666.7 sq meters), with 18 stone stairs leading to the town. Shapo (lit. "sand slope") Valley, originally named Sanpo Valley, was so named because the land in the south of the village consisted of sand.

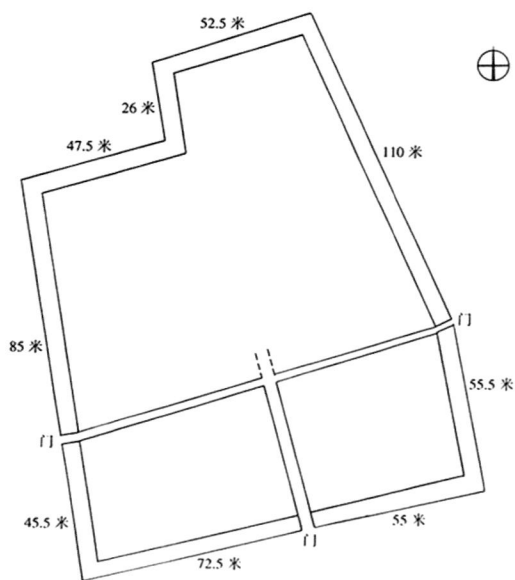

沙坡峪营城平面图（河北文研所测绘）
The floor plan of Shapoyu Yingcheng Garrison (drawn by Hebei Cultural Institute)

沙坡峪长城
The Great Wall at Shapo Valley

沙坡峪长城
The Great Wall at Shapo Valley

沙坡峪长城
The Great Wall at Shapo Valley

沙坡峪关古迹多

沙坡峪关辖地内有25亿年前生成的蛇绿岩遗址，东汉时期的马武坟，明朝初期建的庙坡、平台子等采、冶、铸系列古采矿、冶铁遗址，永乐、宣德两位皇帝驻跸的太子沟，还有古石场、古石营、古石桥、古教场、古马道和抗战名将包森烈士纪念碑。

Many Historical Sites at Shapoyu Valley

Within the jurisdiction of Shapoyu Pass there are many historical sites, including the ruins of ophiolites formed 2.5 billion years ago, Ma Wu's Tomb of the Eastern Han dynasty, ruins of ancient mining and iron-smelting sites such as Miaopo and Pingtaizi established in the early Ming dynasty, and the Prince's Valley where emperors Yongle and Xuande once stayed, as well as an ancient quarry, an ancient stone camp, an ancient stone bridge, an ancient drill ground, an ancient riding track and a monument to General Bao Sen martyred in a battle of resistance against Japanese aggression.

远眺抓髻山
Mount Zhuaji viewed from afar

探秘抓髻山

海拔659.3米的抓髻山，是沙坡峪关东、横拦长城西去的一座险峰。此峰绝壁危耸，恶石高悬，巨坡如滑，古荆遮顶，东来长城临绝壁戛然而止，西去长城到山腰陡生，牧羊人都望崖生怯。卫星云图显示无墙，志书说长城就此断开。抓髻山绝顶无墙？"不，长城在遵化境内不可能因险不筑！"为了匡正史料，接续长城，我们冒险攀上了抓髻山，照片向世人宣告：抓髻山绝顶有长城！

Exploring Mount Zhuaji

Mount Zhuaji, 659.3m above sea level, is a precipitous mountain to the east of Shapoyu Pass blocking the Great Wall extending westward. This peak features precipitous cliffs, steep overhanging rocks, slippery slopes and a top covered with ancient thistles and thorns. The Great Wall from the east abruptly ends by the precipitous cliffs, while the Great Wall running westward abruptly rises from the mountainside. Even goatherds are deterred by the cliffs. No wall is shown on satellite cloud imagery system, and the historical records say that the Great Wall was broken here. Is there no wall on the peak of Mount Zhuaji? "No, it was impossible not to build a section of the wall due to precipitousness!" To rectify historical records and connect the Great Wall, we've ventured to climb up Mount Zhuaji and announced to the world with pictures: on the peak of Mount Zhuaji the Great Wall exists!

上图：
抓髻山顶长城
Picture above:
The Great Wall on the top
of Mount Zhuaji

下图：
抓髻山顶长城
Picture below:
The Great Wall on the top
of Mount Zhuaji

依山傍势 边关独秀——
第五关：冷嘴头关

遵化城西北30华里的兴旺寨乡境内冷嘴头关，是遵化长城东数第五座雄关，是马兰路所辖最东边的第一道关口，永乐年间建，设石崖岭寨、冷嘴头关和龙池寨，完整敌台一座。关城与长城连璧，占地80亩，石城，设南、西、北三门，北门直通长城，驻军190人。口东敌台为万历十四年（1586）增修。

A Pretty Border Town Integrated with Surrounding Mountains— the Fifth Pass: Lengzuitou Pass

Lengzuitou Pass in Xingwangzhai Township 30 *huali* northwest of Zunhua city is the fifth impregnable pass on Zunhua section of the Great Wall from the east, and also the first and easternmost pass governed by the Malanlu Garrison. Established in the Yongle reign, the pass has Shiyaling Stockaded Village, Lengzuitou Pass, Longchi Stockaded Village, and a complete watchtower. The town, connected with the Great Wall, covered an area of 80 *mu*, and was made of stones, having southern, western and northern gates, with the northern gate directly leading to the Great Wall. A total of 190 soldiers were stationed there. The watchtower on the east of the pass was added in the 14th year of the Wanli reign (1586).

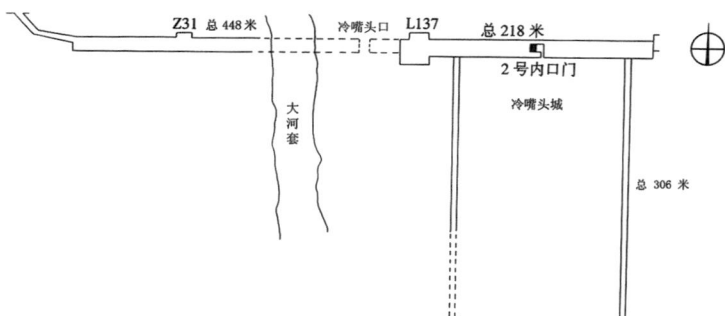

冷嘴头关平面图（河北文研所测绘）
The floor plan of Lengzuitou Pass (drawn by Hebei Cultural Institute)

冷嘴头长城内侧通顶券门
The arched door leading to the Great Wall at Lengzuitou Pass

石崖岭长城
The Great Wall at Shiya Ridge

冷嘴头关
Lengzuitou Pass

冷嘴头的传说

当地人都说"冷嘴头"这个名字还是唐王李世民留下的呢。李世民征东驻跸汤泉，一日他与尉迟敬德去关外霸王寺进香，刚到冷嘴头口子忽一阵凉风吹来，李世民随口道："朕的口好冷！"于是百姓们就管这儿叫作"龙冻口"，年长日久叫白了，叫成了"冷嘴头"。还有的说，冷嘴头南山像龙头，北风一吹瑟瑟作响，似"龙口瑶琴"，便管这儿叫"龙头口"，后来改叫了"冷嘴头"。

冷嘴头长城
The Great Wall at Lengzuitou Pass

The Legend of Lengzuitou

According to local people, the name Lengzuitou was given by Emperor Li Shimin of the Tang dynasty. In his eastern expedition, Li Shimin stayed at Tangquan. One day he offered incense to the Temple of King outside the pass, accompanied by General Yuchi Jingde. The moment they arrived at the pass of Lengzuitou, they met a chilly gust, when Li Shimin spoke without thinking, "How cold my mouth is!" Thereafter, local people called this place Longdongkou (lit. "dragon's mouth frozen"), which evolved into Lengzuitou over time. Some people also say that the southern mountain of Lengzuitou looks like a dragon's head, and gives out a rustle when the northern wind blows, like a lyre at the dragon's mouth. Thus this place was called Longtoukou (lit. "dragon's mouth"), which was later changed to Lengzuitou.

冷嘴头长城
The Great Wall at Lengzuitou Pass

峰转峦回　龙舞群山——
第六关：大安口关

遵化城西北38华里的西下营乡境内大安口关，是遵化长城东数第六座雄关，永乐年间建，设大安口关、井儿峪寨、琵琶峪寨和大安口营（西下营）。此段长城毁坏十分严重，长城已无可见敌台。关城是150米见方的连壁城，南墙设一拱门，门上有匾，书"大安堡"，东有便门，城内有衙门，城南面是校场，驻军174人，马二匹，军械90件。大安口是通往塞外的要隘，1629年八旗军队曾在此破关而入。

A Dragon Dancing on Mountaintops—
the Sixth Pass: Da'ankou Pass

The Da'ankou Pass in the Xixiaying Township 38 *huali* northwest of Zunhua City is the sixth pass from the east on Zunhua section of the Great Wall. Established in the Yongle reign, the Pass had the Da'ankou Pass, the Jing'eryu Stockaded Village, the Pipayu Stockaded Village and the Da'ankou Garrison (Xixia Garrison). This section of the Great Wall has been seriously damaged, without any watchtower extant. The Pass, connected with the Great Wall, covered a square area with a side length of 150 meters. There was an arch gate on the southern wall, on which there was a tablet inscribed with "Da An Bao". There was a side gate in the east. Inside the town there was a government office, and in the south was a drill ground. The pass used to be guarded by 174 soldiers with two horses and 90 weapons. The Da'ankou Pass was a strategic pass to the region beyond the Great Wall, through which the Eight Banners Army once broke and invaded in 1629.

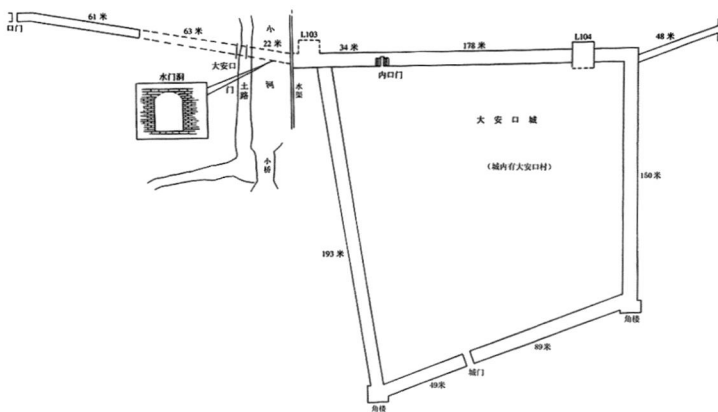

大安口关城平面图（河北文研所测绘）
The floor plan of Da'ankou Pass (drawn by Hebei Cultural Institute)

琵琶峪长城
The Great Wall at the Pipa Valley

琵琶峪长城
The Great Wall at the Pipa Valley

大安口的传说

传洪武六年（1373），戌守长城边务的大将徐达出巡塞外，他站在大安口东山头举目北望，忽见口外有一座酷似皇辇的"轿顶子山"，徐达大喜："这不是我主圣上北征得胜乘辇稳稳进关吗！"他赶紧掐指一算，刚巧是诸葛孔明马前课中的"大安卦"，"此关就叫大安口，以保我朝和圣上永世平安。"远有大明太祖呵护，近有大安雄关扼守，平安富足的大安口人真的好福气呦！

The Legend of Da'ankou

Legend has it that in the 6th year of the Hongwu reign (1373), General Xu Da in charge of border affairs along the Great Wall took a tour of inspection beyond the Great Wall. He looked towards the north on the eastern peak of Da'an Pass and suddenly saw Mount Jiaodingzi which resembled the emperor's carriage. He rejoiced, "Doesn't it mean that our emperor enters the pass in his carriage after the triumph of his northern expedition?" He immediately figured out that it happened to be the Da'an Trigram (lit. "great peace trigram") in Zhuge Kongming's divinatory book. "Let's call this pass Da'ankou, to pray that our dynasty and emperor will be safe and sound forever." With the protection of Emperor Taizu of Ming afar and the impregnable Da'an Pass near, how lucky the people of Da'an Pass are!

大安口关
Da'an Pass

上图：
八十年代大安口关
Picture above:
The Da'an Pass in the 1980s

下图：
八十年代大安口关
Picture below:
The Da'an Pass in the 1980s

蛟龙入水 鲇鱼守关——
第七关：鲇鱼石关

遵化城西北40华里的汤泉乡境内鲇鱼石关，是遵化长城东数第七座雄关，永乐年间建，设沙岭儿寨、鲇鱼石关和鲇鱼石营。此段长城损毁十分严重，长城已无可见敌台。鲇鱼石关因关东长城内侧有一酷似鲇鱼的巨石横卧群山，厮守边关而得名。关城内驻军258人，马五匹。鲇鱼石营设在现鲇鱼池村内，曾有真武阁、钟鼓楼和文武衙门，清乾隆赐营城内一亩三分地种烟，誉满京城，皇封"御石高烟"。此关外通大川，战略位置冲要，常有战事发生。

A Catfish Guarding the Pass—
the Seventh Pass: Nianyushi Pass

Nianyushi Pass in the Tangquan Township 40 *huali* northwest of Zunhua city is the seventh pass from the east on Zunhua section of the Great Wall. Established in the Yongle reign, the pass included the Shaling'er Stockaded Village, Nianyushi Pass and the Nianyushi Garrison. This section of the Great Wall has been seriously damaged, with no watchtower extant. The Nianyushi (lit. "catfish stone") Pass is so named because inside the Great Wall there is a huge rock like a catfish lying on mountains and guarding the border. The pass used to be guarded by 258 soldiers with five horses. The Nianyushi Garrison was set inside the present-day Nianyushi Village, where there used to be a Zhenwu Pavilion, a bell-drum tower and a government office. In the Qianlong reign of the Qing dynasty, 1.3 *mu* land was endowed for tobacco planting, thus the pass was well-known in the capital city. The tobacco planted there was named by the emperor as Tall Tobacco Grown Among Royal Rocks. Leading to a big river, the pass occupies a strategic position, where many battles were fought.

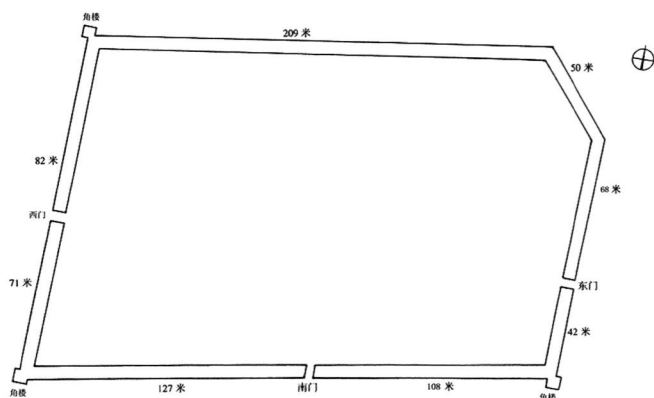

鲇鱼石关城平面图（河北文研所测绘）
The floor plan of Nianyushi Pass (drawn by Hebei Cultural Institute)

鲇鱼石长城
The Great Wall at Nianyushi Pass

长城巨石—— 鲇鱼来游
A huge rock on the Great Wall – A swimming catfish

鲇鱼守关

鲇鱼石关东、长城里侧的山峰上有一地壳剧烈震动时岩浆喷发形成的酷似鲇鱼的岩浆石，每当盛夏，巨大"鲇鱼"便浮在青草如茵的绿波中，与长城相依相伴，牢牢地守候着它身边的这块沃土。据传，当年朱棣巡边到此见关东山脊上有一鲇鱼游来，甚感吉祥，龙颜大悦，说鱼游长城可让百姓常（长城）年（鲇）有余（鱼），他的龙口一开，长城就有了一个叫"鲇鱼石"的关口。

A Catfish Guards the Pass

To the east of Nianyushi Pass, there is a catfish-shaped magma rock on the peak inside the Great Wall, formed by magmatic exhalation when the earth's crust shook violently. In midsummer, the huge "catfish" floats among the green waves of grass, accompanying the Great Wall and guarding the fertile land by its side. It is said that when Zhu Di saw a catfish swim over from the ridge east of the pass on his inspection tour, he considered it a great auspicious sign and was greatly pleased, saying that the fish swimming by the Great Wall could make local people enjoy affluence (the Chinese character of fish is homophonous with that of "affluence") every year (the Chinese character of year is homophonous with that of "catfish"). With the emperor's words, the Great Wall had a pass named Nianyushi.

鲇鱼石关长城
The Great Wall at the Nianyushi Pass

铜墙铁壁上关城

鲇鱼石关外地势开阔平坦，西侧山丘低矮舒缓，既是战略要地，又易攻难守，因此，口西至平山顶东全是两侧包砖、中间灰膏石块浆砌的一等边墙。尽管包砖已被拆走，可中心墙任凭风吹雨打，炮击地震，墙体昂然屹立，400多年坚挺依旧，是遵化段最坚固的长城。

The Strongest Pass of the Great Wall

Beyond Nianyushi Pass the area is spacious, flat and wide, and the hills by its west are low and moderate. It is a strategic place easy to guard and difficult to attack. Therefore, the walls from the west of the pass to the east of Pingshan Peak are all first-grade border walls built with plastered rocks covered with bricks on two sides. Though the bricks were removed, the central walls still stand erect after severe tests of weather, cannon attacks and earthquakes. Remaining rock-solid after over 400 years, this part was the strongest of Zunhua section of the Great Wall.

山崖上垒砌的长城
The Great Wall built on a cliff

长城断开　雄关悲怆——
第八关：马兰关

遵化城西北54华里的马兰峪镇境内马兰关，是遵化长城东数第八座雄关，洪武年间建，设平山寨、马兰关、独松峪寨、峰台岭寨、龙洞峪寨和马兰营。此段长城损毁严重，除了平山顶残台外，长城已无可见敌台。马兰关也叫马兰谷关，志载因一马兰参将守关而名，又说这里盛开马兰而名。马兰关设东西两个与长城连璧的营城，驻军274人，马七匹，军械266件。马兰关外通大道，战略位置十分冲要，多有战事发生。清康熙年间设副将镇守，雍正年间设总兵统辖，建有总兵府、校场、鹿场和官房。

A Sorrowful Pass on a Broken Wall—
the Eighth Pass: Malan Pass

The Malan Pass in the Malanyu Town 54 *huali* northwest of Zunhua city is the eighth pass from the east on Zunhua section of the Great Wall. Established in the Hongwu reign, the pass had the Pingshan Stockaded Village, the Malan Pass, the Dusongyu Stockaded Village, the Fengtailing Stockaded Village, the Longdongyu Stockaded Village and the Malan Garrison. This section of the Great Wall has been seriously damaged, with no watchtower extant, except for a residual tower on the Pingshan Peak. The Malan Pass, also called Malangu Pass, was so named because, according to historical records, a general called Ma Lan once guarded the pass. People also say that it is called Malan Pass because malan flowers bloom here according to another version. The Malan Pass had two garrisons connected with the Great Wall, with 274 soldiers, 7 horses and 266 weapons. The Malan Pass, leading to a main road, occupies a very strategic position, where many battles were fought. In the Kangxi reign of the Qing dynasty, the pass was garrisoned by an assistant general. And in the Yongzheng reign, it was governed by a Commander-in-Chief, housing such establishments as the Commander-in-Chief's office, a drill ground, a deer farm and an officer's residence.

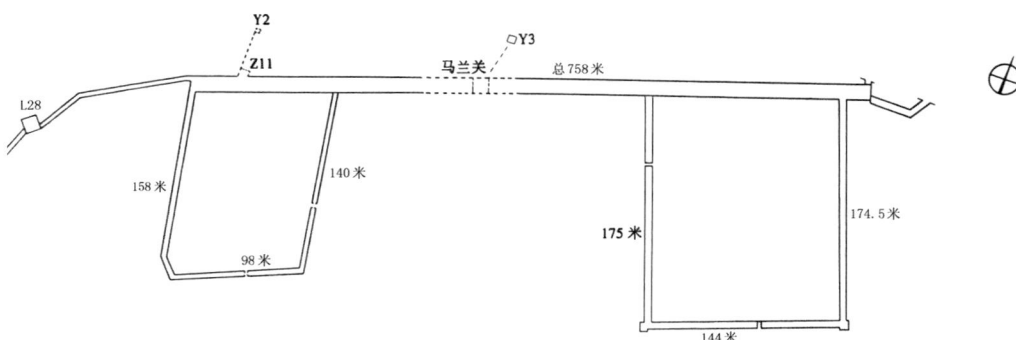

马兰关东营西营平面图（河北文研所测绘）
The floor plan of the East and West Garrisons of Malan Pass (drawn by Hebei Cultural Institute)

被康熙下令拆毁的峰台岭段长城
The Fengtai Ridge Section of the
Great Wall dismantled at
the order of Emperor Kangxi

平山寨长城
The Great Wall at Pingshan Stockaded Village

马兰关
The Malan Pass

马兰路路城马兰峪
Malan Valley of Manlanlu Garrison

马兰关和马兰谷营

马兰关是长城上的雄关要隘，东西两城庙宇繁多，有真武庙、关帝庙、火神庙、药王庙、马王庙、娘娘庙、二郎庙、玉皇庙和华佗殿、满堂佛。清朝建陵后，守陵的绿营最高指挥机关设在这里，雍正元年（1723）因设总兵而改关城为镇城，马兰关遂改叫马兰镇。马兰关南8华里的马兰峪，是明蓟镇十二路的路城，洪武年间建；周长1100米，墙高8.5米。东、南门楼各镶玉石匾额，书"长泰"、"马兰谷营"，东门外有栅楼，书"东藩"。参将把守，驻军1041人，马三十一匹，军械931件。清朝守陵的王公贝勒云集于此，设东西府、义学、书院和多家商铺，繁华异常，号称"小北京"。现被民政部命名为千年古镇。

The Malan Pass and Malangu Garrison

Malan Pass is a strategic pass on the Great Wall, with many temples in its east and west towns, including Zhenwu, Guandi, Huoshen, Yaowang, Mawang, Niangniang, Erlang, and Yuhuang Temples, Huatuo Hall, and Mantang Buddhist Temple. After the Qing mausoleum was built, the highest command of the green battalion guarding the mausoleum was set up there. In the first year of Yongzheng reign (1723), the pass was changed to a garrison as a commander-in-chief was assigned there, and the Malan Pass was renamed the Malan Garrison. Malan Valley, 8 *huali* south of Malan Pass, was one of the 12 *lu* garrisons in the Ming dynasty, established in the Hongwu reign. It had a perimeter of 1,100m, and its walls were 8.5m tall. A jade stone tablet was embedded on each of the southern and eastern gates, on which it was written, "Chang Tai" (ever-lasting peace) and "Ma Lan Gu Ying". Outside the eastern gate there was a gate tower, on which it was written "Dong Fan" (east fence). The pass was guarded by a *canjiang* (lit. "staff general") leading 1,041 soldiers with 31 horses and 931 weapons. Princes and dukes guarding the mausoleum gathered here in the Qing dynasty. It was called Lesser Beijing as it was very prosperous, boasting with the eastern and western mansions, a community-run school, an academy and many stores. It has now been rated as a 1000-year-old ancient town by the Ministry of Civil Affairs.

马兰关东营
The East Garrison of Malan Pass

马兰关西营
The West Garrison of Malan Pass

马兰关外圆楼

由于马兰关的战略位置十分冲要，为御敌，特在关外1华里处的高岗上设一圆形哨楼。楼基八层，基上为砖砌圆形空心敌台，正南有门，四周设砖拱箭窗，台顶设楼橹，是我市长城外侧唯一一座圆形敌台。一百年前美国探险家盖洛到达马兰关时，顾不得进关拜访迎候他的八旗长官，就迫不及待地去拍奇特圆楼，拍完他激动地大喊："莱法耶特学院（盖洛母校），欢呼吧！"被盖洛吼得一脸迷茫的晚清旗人，没等这位洋人走远也都鹦鹉学舌地吼起了这句到头不到脑的洋话。

The Round Tower
beyond the Malan Pass

Since the Malan Pass occupied a very strategic position, a round sentry tower was set up on a tall peak 1 *huali* beyond the pass to resist the enemy. The base of the tower was of eight stories, on which a round hollow brick watchtower was built. There was a gate in the due south, surrounded with brick arch arrow holes. On the top of the tower was a movable wooden watchtower. This is the only round watchtower on the outer side of the Great Wall in Zunhua. One hundred years ago, when the US explorer William Edgar Geil reached the Malan Pass, he went to take pictures of the strange round tower, before meeting the officers waiting for him. Afterwards, he shouted excitedly, "Lafayette, cheers!" The Qing officers puzzled with Geil's behavior also parroted this nonsense foreign remark before the foreigner went afar.

堂子山上永旺塔

群山环顾的马兰峪形如碧波荡舟，舟有樯则行稳，则民安，则财旺。万历九年（1581）蓟镇总兵戚继光依相士议，以"毋伤军财，毋劳军力，我工我鸠，我贳我集，石凿必坚，砖陶必固，相厥土宜，诹日起事"为原则，在镇南堂子山建起了高17米、腰砌八棱、顶设七檐、角坠风铃、雕花刻草的玲珑宝塔。430年过去了，永旺塔让马兰峪如凭樯大舟，扬帆破浪，稳稳前行。

The Yongwang Pagoda on Mount Tangzi

Malan Valley surrounded by mountains looks like a ship sailing among green waves. A ship sails stably with a mast, and then people will enjoy peace and prosperity. In the 9th year of the Wanli reign (1581), Commander-in-Chief Qi Jiguang of Jizhen Garrison consulted fortune-teller and built an exquisite pagoda with eight ridges and seven eaves, wind chimes and engraved flowers and grass. In doing this, he followed the principle of raising human and financial resources by themselves, using solid stones, making firm bricks, properly digging earth and building on auspicious days, instead of using money or manpower reserved for military. For over 430 years the Yonguang Pagoda protected Malan Valley and brought people there peace and stablility.

上图：
永旺塔顶部
Picture above:
Top of Yongwang Pagoda

下图：
远眺永旺塔
Picture below:
Yongwang Pagoda viewed from afar

长城翻越平山顶

万里长城跃出上关湖，蜿蜒西行，爬上了京东名峰平山顶。远远望去，万顷碧波中的古长城犹如巨大项链，串起如珠山峰，平山顶突兀其中。登上平山顶，顶平如砥，古树蓊郁，花香扑鼻。顶北有墙，墙上有楼，楼前有庙，庙旁有井，井南有碾，碾下有洞，洞内有仙。康熙二十年（1681）康熙登临此山，饱览关山，龙心大悦，随口颂道"养在闺中人未识"，敕封此山为"麒麟山"。游上关湖，登古长城，攀麒麟山，让我们都来找一下做皇帝的感觉吧！

The Great Wall Jumped over Pingshan Peak

The Great Wall jumps out of Shangguan Lake to wind westward and climb over Pingshan Peak, a famous peak in the east of Beijing. Viewed from afar, the ancient Great Wall among a vast expanse of green forests is like a huge necklace stringing together pearl-like peaks, of which Pingshan Peak stands out. On Pingshan Peak, we can see that the top is as flat as a whetstone, with luxuriant ancient trees and fragrant flowers around. In the north of the peak there is a wall, on which stands a tower. The tower has a temple in its front, by which there is a well. South of the well is a roller, under which there is a cave. Inside the cave lives an immortal. In the 20th year of Kangxi reign (1681), Emperor Kangxi visited the Guanshan Peak. Delighted by the beautiful scenery, he spoke highly of the mountain and named it Mount Kylin. Let's visit Shangguan Lake, climb the ancient Great Wall and ascend Mount Kylin to experience the feeling of the emperor.

平山顶
Pingshan Peak

清东陵和康熙下令拆毁的峰台岭至独松峪段长城遗址
Eastern Mausoleum of the Qing dynasty and the ruins of the section
of the Great Wall from the Fengtai Ridge to Dusong Valley dismantled upon the order of Emperor Kangxi

康熙拆长城

雄伟的长城翻过平山顶，先向西北弯个大弯后直奔西南的马兰关、独松峪、峰台岭、凤凰岭而去。清王朝定鼎中原后，顺治皇帝选峰台岭前的风水宝地为万年吉地。顺治十八年（1661）皇帝驾崩，康熙为父皇筹建陵寝时以长城压龙脉为由下令"陵后长城自马兰关第二台以西，龙洞峪第二台以东，俱系龙脉所在，不宜有城，因以撤焉"。是康熙让万里长城断开了一个15华里的大口子。

Kangxi Pulled Down the Great Wall

The majestic Great Wall crosses the Pingshan Peak and makes a great turn towards the northwest before it directly runs toward the Malan Pass, the Dusong Valley, the Fengtai Ridge and Fenghuang Ridge in the southwest. After the Qing dynasty was settled down in the Central Plains, Emperor Shunzhi selected a geomantic treasure land in front of the Fengtai Ridge as his tomb site. When Shunzhi passed away in the 18th year of his reign (1661), Emperor Kangxi, seeing that the Great Wall pressed on the dragon's vein when his father's tomb was built, ordered to pull down the section of the Great Wall from the second watchtower from the Malan Pass in the west to the second watchtower of the Longdong Valley in the east. Because of it, there appeared a 15-*huali*-wide gap on the Great Wall.

① ② ③ 康熙下令拆毁的
独松峪段长城遗址
Ruins of the Great Wall at
Dusong Valley dismantled upon
the order of Emperor Kangxi

④ 康熙下令拆毁的
峰台岭段长城遗址
Ruins of the Great Wall at
Fengtai Ridge dismantled upon
the order of Emperor Kangxi

朴拙沧桑 蜿蜒西去——
第九关：宽佃峪关

遵化城西北60华里的东陵乡境内宽佃峪关，是遵化长城东数第九座雄关，也是与蓟县搭边的最西边的一道雄关。永乐年间建，设宽佃峪关和饿老婆顶寨。此段长城毁坏十分严重，城上已无可见敌台。宽佃峪关城也就是现在的东陵乡楦门子，是我市目前保存最完好的一座关城。驻军203人，马二匹，军械167件。出楦门子往北就是清朝守陵的哨所一拨子、二拨子、三拨子、……八拨子。

A Dilapidated Wall
Winding Westward—
the Ninth Pass: Kuandianyu Pass

The Kuandianyu Pass in the Dongling Township that is 60 *huali* northwest of Zunhua city is the ninth pass from the east on Zunhua section of the Great Wall, which is also the westernmost pass bordering Ji County. Established in the Yongle reign, the pass encompassed Kuandianyu Pass and Elaopoding Stockaded Village. This section of the Great Wall has been seriously damaged, without any watchtower extant. The Kuandianyu Pass is the present-day Xuanmenzi Village of Dongling Township, which is the best preserved pass in Zunhua. It used to be guarded by 203 soldiers with 2 horses and 167 weapons. North of the Xuanmenzi Village were 8 watchhouses of the Qing mausoleum, from No. 1 to No. 8.

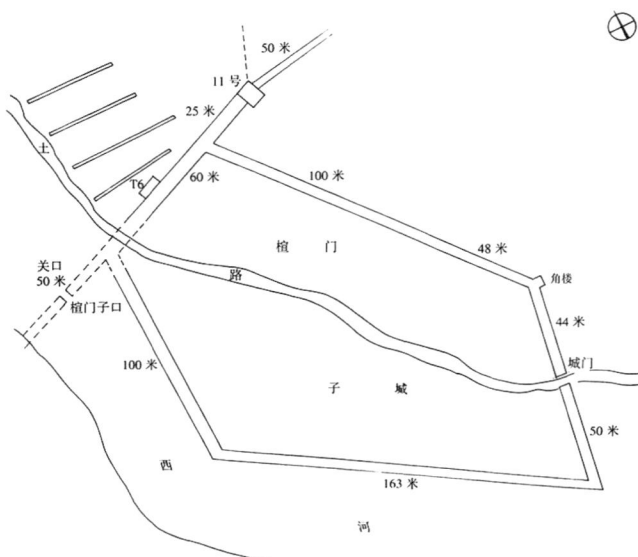

宽佃峪关城楦门子平面图（河北文研所测绘）

The floor plan of Xuanmenzi of Kuandianyu Pass (drawn by Hebei Cultural Institute)

凤凰岭长城
The Great Wall at Fenghuang Ridge

凤凰岭长城
The Great Wall at Fenghuang Ridge

宽佃峪关
Kuandianyu Pass

凤凰岭马武石
Mawu Rock at Fenghuang Ridge

马武石和破城子

公元25年，刘秀派大将马武追流寇于俊糜（遵化）大破之，遂将河北平定。为感念马武的功劳，刘秀登基后特在凤凰岭点化一巨石为"马武石"，向东永远护佑俊糜。马武石下便是遵化31道关寨中最西边的一道关寨——饿老婆顶寨，寨堡后曰"破城子"，抗战时期代称"小上海"并沿用至今。寨堡遗迹尚存，曾驻军54人。

长城艰难地爬上饿老婆顶筑一敌台后，分成两岔，一向西北延伸约200米，筑一哨台后便戛然而止；一向西南再折向西北奔蓟县黄崖关龙腾而去，在895米的凤凰岭顶峰筑一遵化长城最高敌台。登台四望，京津冀数百里山川沃野尽收眼底，遵化138华里明长城至此全部结束。

Mawu Rock and Pochengzi Stockaded Village

In 25 AD, Liu Xiu dispatched General Ma Wu to pursue rebel bands and thoroughly defeat them in Junmi (present-day Zunhua), thus pacifying Hebei. To commemorate Ma Wu's contributions, Liu Xiu, after ascending the throne, named a huge rock at Fenghuang Ridge after Mawu, which would symbolically protect Junmi in the east forever. Under the Mawu Rock is Elaopoding Stockaded Village, the westernmost one of the 31 in Zunhua, which was later called Pochengzi. It was also called Little Shanghai during the War of Resistance against Japanese Aggression, a name used till now. The ruins of the stockade still remain, where 54 soldiers were once stationed.

The Great Wall, after being extended to a watchtower on the Elaopo Peak with great difficulty, has two branches, one extending about 200m northwestwards and abruptly ending at a sentry tower, while the other running southwestwards and then turning northwest towards the Huangya Pass in Ji County, reaching the tallest watchtower on Zunhua section of the Great Wall at the top of Fenghuang Ridge which has an altitude of 895m. The watchtower commands a view of mountains and fields of several hundred *li* in Beijing, Tianjin and Hebei. And Zunhua section of the Ming Great Wall running 138 *huali* ends up here.

上图：
凤凰岭长城
Picture above:
The Great Wall at Fenghuang Ridge

下图：
破城子寨堡
Picture below:
Pochengzi Stockade

雄踞蓟镇唱大风

公元前196年，大汉开国皇帝刘邦荣归故里，置酒沛宫，击筑高歌："大风起兮云飞扬，威加海内兮归故乡，安得猛士兮守四方！"

两千多年来，遵化长城扼外虏，阻日寇，震顽敌，犹如巨人，高唱《大风》，雄踞蓟镇。

The Great Wall Majestically Protected Jizhen Garrison

In 196 BC, Liu Bang, the founding emperor of the Han dynasty, returned to his hometown in glory. He set up a banquet in the palace and composed a poem while striking a *zhu* musical instrument, "A big wind rises, and clouds are driven away./ Home am I now, and the world is under my sway./ Where are brave men to guard the four frontiers today!"

Over more than 2000 years, Zunhua section of the Great Wall has carried forward the spirit of the *Song of the Big Wind* and been protecting Jizhen Garrison by resisting enemies such as northern tribes and Japanese invaders.

洪山口长城
The Great Wall at Hongshan Pass

白枣峪长城

The Great Wall at Baizao Valley

遵化长城战事多

从洪武元年（1368）到崇祯十六年（1643）的275年中，明朝共发生过大小战争579次（《中国军事史》）。是连绵不断的残酷军事战争铸就了举世无双的万里长城。仅遵化长城沿线就发生过建文元年（1399）朱允炆抄剿朱棣的战争、正德二年（1507）武宗大败兀良哈的战争，正德四年（1509）、十年（1515），嘉靖二十四年（1545）、二十九年（1550）、三十四年（1555）、三十八年（1559）分别发生过鞑靼、朵颜、土蛮等破长城掠遵化的战争。此前，还发生过曹操征讨乌桓、隋文帝平北、唐王征东等战争。

Numerous Wars on Zunhua Section of the Great Wall

During the 275 years from the first year of the Hongwu reign (1368) to the 16th year of the Chongzhen reign (1643), a total of 579 wars of different scale took place in the Ming dynasty (*The Military History of China*). It was the ceaseless cruel wars that helped to forge the peerless Great Wall. Along Zunhua section of the Great Wall alone, the following wars occurred: the war of Zhu Yunwen suppressing Zhu Di in the first year of the Jianwen reign (1399), the war of Emperor Wuzong defeating Uriankhai in the 2nd year of the Zhengde reign (1507), and wars launched by northern tribes such as Tartar, Duoyan and Tuman breaking through the Great Wall to plunder Zunhua in the 4th year (1509) and the 10th year (1515) of the Zhengde reign, the 24th year (1545), the 29th year (1550), the 34th year (1555), and the 38th year (1559) of the Jiajing reign. Earlier wars included Cao Cao's expedition to Wuhuan, Emperor Wen of Sui's suppression of northern uprising, and the eastern expedition in the Tang dynasty, etc.

曹操遵化出奇兵

东汉末年，军阀逐鹿中原，居辽西的乌桓日渐强盛，他们南下攻城掠地，为河北一带严重边患。建安十年（205），曹操摧毁了袁绍在河北的统治，袁绍呕血而死，其子袁尚、袁熙北逃乌桓后常入塞为害。南有荆襄的刘表、刘备，北有乌桓和袁氏兄弟，腹背受敌的曹操，采纳谋士郭嘉之策，于建安十二年（207）夏率师北征，五月至无终（遵化），七月遇大水，傍海大道不通。后又接受无终人田畴建议，佯装退兵，绕道遵化城西南的徐无山（《遵化州志》），出奇兵于燕塞，经白檀（宽城）过平冈（凌源）直捣乌桓的老巢柳城（辽阳），大败乌军，俘敌20万人。曹操七月出塞，九月沿傍海大道得胜而归时，登临碣石，吟咏了千古绝唱《观沧海》。

Cao Cao Had an Ingenious Military Move in Zunhua

In the last years of the Eastern Han dynasty, warlords fought for control of the Central Plains. Wuhuan in western Liaoning gradually became powerful, and invaded southern land, posing a serious threat to regions around Hebei. In the 10th year of the Jian'an reign (205), Cao Cao overthrew the rule of Yuan Shao in Hebei. Yuan Shao died of blood spitting, and his sons Yuan Shang and Yuan Xi fled northward to Wuhuan, frequently entering the border to make troubles. With Liu Biao and Liu Bei in the Jingzhou-Xiangyang areas of the south, and Wuhuan and the Yuan brothers in the north, Cao Cao was attacked from all sides. He adopted the suggestion of his adviser Guo Jia to lead an army for a northern expedition in the summer of the 12th year of the Jian'an reign (207). He arrived in Wuzhong (present-day Zunhua) in May, and met a flood in July, obstructing the main roads by sea. Later Cao accepted Tian Chou's suggestion and pretended to retreat. He made a detour around Mount Xuwu in the southwest of Zunhua (*The Annals of Zunhua Prefecture*), took an ingenious military move at the Yan border, and passed Baitan (preset-day Kuancheng) and Pinggang (present-day Lingyuan) to directly attack the headquarters of Wuhuan, i.e. Liucheng (present-day Liaoyang), utterly defeating the Wuhuan army and capture 200,000 enemies. Cao Cao, who departed for the border areas in July and returned triumphant along coastal roads, ascended the Jieshi Rock and composed his masterpiece *Viewing the Boundless Sea*.

三道岭长城
The Great Wall at the Sandao Ridge

后杖子长城
The Great Wall at the Houzhangzi Village

隋文帝遵化战突厥

隋开皇三年（583），突厥首领沙钵略可汗联合前北齐营州刺史高宝宁突入遵化以东各关隘，隋文帝遂派杨爽为行军元帅率20万大军大败突厥，派幽州总管阴寿出塞抄杀高宝宁老巢，收复长城内外大片失地，隋朝北部边境趋于安宁。（《长城百科全书》）

朱棣四下遵化退官兵

朱元璋四子朱棣被封燕王，领北京、永平和保定。建文帝欲削藩朱棣。建文元年（1399）七月，"庚寅，遵化卫指挥蒋玉言，都督刘真、陈亨，都指挥使卜万引大宁兵（官兵），出松亭关，驻沙河，将攻遵化。"朱棣带兵急援，将官兵打退关外，并离间朝廷下狱了卜万。九月，淮阴侯吴高，都指挥使耿瓛、杨文率辽东兵围永平，朱棣出遵化驱官兵。建文二年（1400）、三年（1401）辽东总兵杨文率师围永平，朱棣出遵化救之（《建文朝野汇编》）。"靖难之役"中兀良哈三卫与朱棣合作打败朝廷，顺势南下入滦河、辽河套，直逼京东。朱棣登基后又拱手把大宁等卫让给兀良哈，给日后的大明留下了巨大隐患。

Emperor Wen of Sui Dynasty Defeated Turkic Troops in Zunhua

In the 3rd year of the Kaihuang period of Sui dynasty (583), the Turkic leader Shabenliao Khan broke into passes east of Zunhua in alliance with Gao Baoning, former prefectural governor of Yingzhou in the Northern Qi dynasty. Emperor Wen appointed Yang Shuang as the general to lead an army of 200,000 soldiers to utterly defeat the Turks, and dispatched Governor Yin Shou of the Youzhou Prefecture to go beyond the Great Wall to destroy Gao Baoning's headquarters. A large area of lost territory inside and outside the Great Wall was thus recovered, and the northern border of the Sui dynasty became peaceful. (*An Encyclopedia of the Great Wall*)

Zhu Di Expelled Government Troops from Zunhua for Four Times

Zhu Di, the fourth son of Zhu Yuanzhang, was conferred the title of Prince of Yan, governing Beijing, Yongping and Baoding. Emperor Jianwen intended to weaken the power of Zhu Di. In the seventh lunar month of the first year of the Jianwen reign (1399), "Jiang Yuyan, Commander of Zunhua Wei, governors Liu Zhen and Chen Heng, and Commander-in-Chief Bu Wan led troops in Daning (government troops) to go beyond the Songting Pass, and were then stationed at Shahe, about to attack Zunhua." Zhu Di came to rescue with his troops, expelling the government troops beyond the pass. Also he sowed discord in the court to have Bu Wan imprisoned. In September, Marquis of Huaiyin Wu Gao, Commanders-in-Chief Geng Huan and Yang Wen led Liaodong troops to besiege Yongping, and Zhu Di left for Zunhua to expel the government troops. In the 2nd year (1400) and 3rd year (1401) of the Jianwen reign, Liaodong Commander-in-Chief Yang Wen led an army to besiege Yong Ping, and Zhu Di left for Zunhua to rescue the city (*Historical Materials on the Court and the Commonalty of the Jianwen Reign*). During the Jingnan Campaign, the three *wei* units of Uriankhai and Zhu Di cooperated to defeat the court, and took advantage of the opportunity to go south to the Luanhe and the Liaohe river basins, threatening the east of the capital. After ascending the throne, Zhu Di surrendered Daning and other *wei* regions to Uriankhai, leaving a serious hazard to the Ming dynasty.

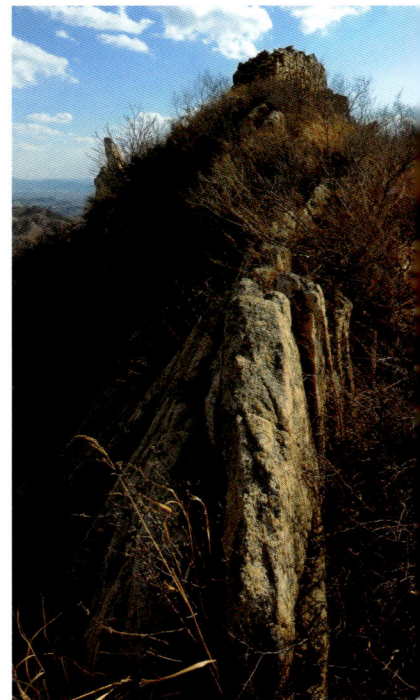

后杖子长城
The Great Wall at the Houzhangzi Village

宣德东征赞遵化

兀良哈三卫得势于大宁（内蒙宁城一带）内徙，时常侵扰中原。有鉴于此，明宣宗于宣德三年（1428）遂出遵化亲征兀良哈于喜峰口外宽河之地。"上命分铁骑为两翼夹击之。上亲射其前锋三人，殪之。两翼飞矢如雨，射虏，虏不能胜。继而神机铳迭发，虏人马死者大半，余悉溃走。上以数百骑直前。虏观黄龙旗，知上亲在也，悉下马罗拜请降，皆生俘之。遂获虏牲口、驼马、牛羊、辎重。"（《明宣宗实录》）宣宗得胜回师驻跸遵化时，发现这里乡风淳朴，民心向学，"五子登科"的窦氏家族又出遵化，遂在西大寺扩建完一寺庙时，特御笔赐匾"广慧"以颂遵化。

廖家峪寨长城
The Great Wall at the Liaojiayu Stockaded Village

Emperor Xuande Commended Zunhua in His Eastern Expedition

The three *wei* units of Uriankhai moved inward by conquering of Daning (along Ningcheng of Inner Mongolia), and often intruded into the Central Plains. In light of this situation, in the 3rd year of the Xuande reign (1428), Emperor Xuanzong of Ming dynasty went on an expedition via Zunhua and fought Uriankhai along the Kuanhe River beyond the Xifeng Pass. "The emperor ordered that the cavalry be divided into two wings to attack the enemy from two sides. The emperor shot three vanguards to death. The two wings shot flying arrows like raindrops against the enemy. And with the following use of blunderbusses, the majority of the enemy's soldiers and horses were killed, while the rest all fled. The emperor pursued them with several hundred cavalrymen. As the enemy saw the Yellow Dragon Banner, which suggested the presence of the emperor, they all got off horses to surrender and all of them were captured alive. The enemy's draught animals, camels, horses, cattle, sheep and supplies were all captured." (*Records of Emperor Xuanzong of Ming Dynasty*) When he stayed in Zunhua after the triumph, Emperor Xuanzong appreciated the plain folk customs and the pursuit of scholarship there, where the Dou's family "with all five sons succeeding in imperial examinations" lived. So the emperor personally inscribed a tablet with "Guang Hui" (lit. "Wide Wisdom") eulogizing Zunhua for a building extended from the Xida Temple.

马永设伏洪山口

蓟镇第二十八任总兵马永，遵化东胜右卫人（《遵化州志》），初袭职金吾左卫指挥使，正德年间奉命守遵化时，因在马兰关御敌勇猛而升为参将。嘉靖元年（1522）朵颜部首领把儿孙率敌犯边，马永在洪山口巧设伏击阵，不但杀敌无算，还斩杀了朵颜一员大将，从此把儿孙不敢再擅扰边塞，因功升为右都督，景忠山下建有马公祠。

Ma Yong Set up an Ingenious Ambush at Hongshan Pass

Ma Yong, the 28th Commander-in-Chief of Jizhen Garrison, was a native of the Dongsheng Right Wei of Zunhua (*The Annals of Zunhua Prefecture*) and first inherited the title of commander of the Jinwu Left Wei. He was promoted to be a *canjiang* officer for his valiant resistance of the enemy at the Malan Pass when he was ordered to defend Zunhua in the Zhengde reign. In the first year of the Jiajing reign (1522), Ba'ersun, the chief of the Duoyan Tribe, led a troop to attack the border. Ma Yong set up an ingenious ambush at the Hongshan Pass, killing numerous enemy soldiers, including a general of the Duoyan Tribe. From then on, Ba'ersun no longer dared to invade the border area. Ma Yong was thus promoted to Lieutenant Viceroy. Later, the Temple of Duke Ma was built at the foot of Mount Jingzhong.

戚继光五战董狐狸

隆庆二年（1568）腊月，朵颜酋长董狐狸和侄子长昂聚众会州准备进犯遵迁长城隘口，刚到蓟镇不久的戚继光率车兵策应，痛击犯敌，董狐狸险被俘。万历元年（1573）二月董狐狸又来犯边，戚继光率兵堵截，斩首3级，余敌负伤逃窜。四、五月，董狐狸勾结土蛮进犯桃林口、界岭口，戚继光命游击王轸退敌，董狐狸丢下部众15人、马53匹、骡2头、器物369件仓皇逃命。六、七月春防刚过，董狐狸乘客兵已撤又犯边于遵化等关隘，戚继光率兵迎战，斩6人，获马12匹和大量器械。万历三年（1575）正月董狐狸和长秃（酋长）又犯边遵迁，戚继光主动出击，去边150里，活捉长秃。三月初一，董狐狸率部众240人扣关请罪，求赎长秃，盟誓朵颜世代内附，永不犯边。（《戚少保年谱耆编》）

洪山口关
Hongshan Pass

Qi Jiguang Combated Dong Huli for Five Times

In the 12th lunar month of the 2nd year of the Longqing reign (1568), Dong Huli, the chief of the Duoyan Tribe, and his nephew Chang'ang gathered a gang in preparation to invade a pass of the Great Wall in Zunhua and Qian'an. Qi Jiguang just arriving in Jizhen Garrison led chariot soldiers to give a heavy blow to the invading enemy, with Dong Huli almost being captured. In the second lunar month of the first year of the Wanli reign(1573), Dong Huli invaded the border again. Qi Jiguang led a troop to block them, beheading three of them, while the rest fled bewounded. In the fourth and fifth months, Dong Huli colluded with local barbarians to invade the Taolin Pass and the Jieling Pass. Qi Jiguang ordered the head of guerrilla warfare Wang Zhen to defeat the enemy. Dong Huli escaped for life leaving 15 of his men, 53 horses, two mules and 369 weapons behind. In the sixth and seventh lunar months, when the spring defense was just over, Dong Huli invaded passes in Zunhua and other places again after knowing that external soldiers were removed. Qi Jiguang led troops to fight against the enemy, killing 6 soldiers, capturing 12 horses and numerous weapons. In the 3rd year of the Wanli reign (1575), DongHuli and Changtu (tribal chief) invaded the border town Zunhua and Qian'an again. Qi Jiguang proactively attacked them and captured Changtu alive 150 *li* away from the border. On March 1, Dong Huli led a team of 240 people to ask for punishment and request the release of Changtu, pledging that the Duoyan tribe would submit to the rule of Ming and never invade the border again. (*A Chronicle of Qi Jiguang's Life*)

左图：廖家峪长城
The picture on the left: The Great Wall at Liaojia Valley

当年戚继光阅兵之地——汤堡平原
The venue where Qi Jiguang inspected the military parade—the Tangbao Plain

戚继光汤泉大阅兵

隆庆六年（1572）十一月，总兵戚继光调蓟镇12万将士，分12路，在汤泉以南20平方公里的开阔地，进行了一次近战、夜战、步战、车战、阵战、墙战和伏击等20天的实战演习，兵部右侍郎汪道昆、蓟辽总督刘应节、顺天巡抚杨兆等朝廷和地方要员观摩了盛大军演。这次名载史册的实战大阅兵高扬了明朝军威，使得残元势力多年不敢窥视中原。

Qi Jiguang's Military Parade at Tangquan

In November of the 6th year of the Longqing reign (1572), Commander-in-Chief Qi Jiguang dispatched 120,000 soldiers in 12 columns to conduct a 20-day-long combat exercise with live ammunition including close combat, night combat, infantry combat, chariot combat, arrayed combat, wall combat and ambush etc. on an open land of 20 km² south of Tangquan. Important court and local officials such as Right Assistant Minister of War Wang Daokun, Ji-Liao Governor Liu Yingjie, and Shuntian Grand Coordinator Yang Zhao watched the grand parade. This grand military parade recorded in historical books boosted the military authority of the Ming dynasty and deterred residual Yuan forces from coveting the Central Plains.

骷石驱虏

相传万历六年（1578）五月，鞑靼一万骑兵扎营鲇鱼石关外百里准备犯边，敌寇慑于戚继光治军威严不敢轻进，夜里派仨暗探准备摸进关内刺探军情。他们避开正关，顺口东攀崖而上，谁知快到长城时，突然一怪物挡住去路，举火一看，只见一巨大骷髅正对他们怒目而视。"啊 —— 鬼！"突如其来的惨叫，吓得后面正在攀崖的暗探顺势坠下山谷，摔得脑浆迸裂。打头的两个探兵没等缓过神来，就成了俘虏。一万敌军远远窥伺十日，见明军严阵以待，怯阵不战自退。

鲇鱼石关外骷石
Skeleton-Shaped Stone
outside the Nianyushi Pass

A Skeleton-Shaped Stone Expelled Tartar Spies

In the fifth lunar month of the 6th year of the Wanli reign (1578), a Tartar cavalry of 10,000 soldiers was stationed 100 *li* outside the Nianyushi Pass ready for attacking the border. Deterred by Qi Jiguang's military power, they dared not intrude rashly. Three spies were dispatched at night to slip into the border to pry into the military situation. Evading the regular pass, they climbed up cliffs east of the pass. But the moment they approached the Great Wall, they were blocked by a strange thing. When they observed it by the light of a fire, they saw a huge skeleton glaring at them. "Ah—ghost!" The unexpected screech by the first two spies frightened the third who was climbing a cliff behind so much that he slid down and fell to his death. The leading two spies, before they were captured, realized what had happened. The 10,000 enemy soldiers were on watch for ten days far away. But deterred by the troops of the Ming who were ready to combat, the enemy soilders retreated without fighting.

洪山口关
The Hongshan Pass

皇太极破关犯京城

崇祯二年（1629）十月，皇太极率领十万大军在范文程引导下绕道蒙古喀喇沁伐明，连破龙井关、洪山口、大安口后，在城内进士贾维钥和佥事马思恭 的内应下，攻进遵化城，巡抚王元雅自杀。皇太极留范文程及800兵丁守卫遵化，继续挥师西进，破三河，掠通州，下顺义，直逼北京城下，大战德胜门、广渠门、永定门，致使许多将领战死，回师时又攻陷了香河、滦州、迁安、永平四城，饱掠四个月之后才从迁安冷口撤出，史称"己巳之变"。

遵化归清

崇祯十七年（1644）三月，闯王李自成派李廷环等人来监理遵化公务。同月，清军围攻遵化，明巡抚宋权在北门设伏诱杀义军官员献城迎清，遵化遂归于清。

Huang Taiji Broke into Passes to Invade Beijing

In the tenth lunar month of the 2nd year of the Chongzhen reign (1629), Huang Taiji led an army of 100,000 soldiers to attack the Ming dynasty under the guidance of Fan Wencheng and took a detour through Harkin of Mongol. After breaking through the Longjing Pass, the Hongshan Pass and the Da'ankou Pass successively, the army entered Zunhua city with the coordination of Jia Weiyao, a *jinshi* scholar, and Commander Ma Sigong. Grand Coordinator Wang Yuanya committed suicide. Leaving Fan Wencheng and 800 soldiers behind to guard Zunhua, Huang Taiji continued to march westward with his army, breaking into Sanhe, plundering Tongzhou, invading Shunyi, and directly threatening Beijing by fighting at the Desheng Gate, the Guangqu Gate and the Yongding Gate. This caused the death of many officers. In his triumphant return, Huang Taiji captured Xianghe, Luanzhou, Qian'an and Yongping, and didn't retreat from the Lengkou Pass of Qian'an until after four months' plunder. This was called the Jisi Incident in history.

Zunhua's Subjection to Qing Dynasty

In the third lunar month of the 17th year of the Chongzhen reign (1644), Li Zicheng, nicknamed Dashing King, dispatched Li Tinghuan and other people to supervise over the affairs in Zunhua. In the same month, the Qing army besieged Zunhua. Governor Song Quan of Ming Dynasty set up an ambush at the northern gate to kill officers of the rebel army and offered the city to Qing. Thus Zunhua was subjected to Qing.

永远的伤疤　永世的痛

1933年3月16—18日，从喜峰口败退下来的日军在关东军司令武藤信义的指挥下，出动了50多架次飞机、十数门山野炮、数十挺轻重机枪和近万名日寇、关东军对我罗文峪一线长城狂轰滥炸，5座关口为之变形，37华里长城被炸坍损，64座敌台垮塌。三山垂泪，两川怒吼，摧而不垮的遵化长城是日本军国主义留给中华民族的永远的伤疤，永世的痛。

Perpetual Scars and Permanent Pains

During March 16-18, 1933, the Japanese army retreating from their defeat at the Xifeng Pass, under the command of Nobuyoshi Mut, a Japanese Commander of the Japanese Kwantung Army, dispatched over 50 planes, over ten cannons and several dozens of light and heavy machine guns, as well as nearly 10,000 Japanese soldiers and Kwantong soldiers to bomb the Great Wall along Luowen Valley. Five passes were deformed, 37 *li* of the wall crumbled, and 64 watchtowers broken down. Mountains shed tears and rivers roared. Zunhua section of the Great Wall, which didn't collapse despite serious damage, testifies to the permanent scars and pains left by the Japanese militarists to the Chinese nation.

被炸后的罗文峪敌台
Luowenyu Watchtower after bombing

左图：
大安口村84岁的杨瑞合世代蜗居杨家楼敌台，1942年日寇清剿，敌台被炸，他家被赶进了日寇制造的"人圈"，受尽折磨，八路军救他们逃离虎口。

The picture on the left:
The family of Yang Ruihe, an 84-year-old man at the Da'ankou Village, lived in the Yangjialou watchtower for generations. In 1942, the watchtower was bombed by Japanese invaders, and his family was driven to a "human pen" made by Japanese invaders, where they were tortured. It was the Eighth Route Army that rescued them.

洪山口长城
The Great Wall at the Hongshan Pass

把我们的血肉筑成我们新的长城

1933年3月，日本帝国主义靠飞机大炮的狂轰滥炸破关而进，自此，遵化和长城遭受了强盗铁蹄长达十二年多的蹂躏、践踏和摧残。此间，日寇在遵化制造了鲁家峪、莫屯等29起惨案，151个村的3.1万人被赶进"无人区"里的"人圈"，全县总伤亡128707人，3319人死于日寇刺刀下，27476间房子被毁，632公斤黄金被掠采。不屈不挠的遵化人民，不畏强盗，同仇敌忾，奋起反抗，以血肉之躯铸成了抵御外虏、歼灭倭寇的钢铁长城，最终和全国人民一道把日寇赶出了中国。

Building the New Great Wall with Our Flesh and Blood

In March 1933, Japanese imperialists broke into our border with savage bombings by aircrafts and cannons. From then on, Zunhua and the Great Wall went through over 12 years' devastation, and humiliation by the robbers. During this period, Japanese invaders perpetrated 29 massacres at the Lujia Valley and Motun in Zunhua. A total of 31,000 people of 151 villages were driven into the "human pen" in the "no man's area". The total casualties in the county amounted to 128,707. In particular, 3,319 people were killed, 27,476 houses were destroyed, and 632kg of gold was plundered. The people in Zunhua shared bitter hatred against the enemy and jointly resisted Japanese aggression. They built a "great wall" to resist foreign invasion with their blood and flesh, and finally drove the Japanese invaders out of China together with other people across the country.

大刀向鬼子们的头上砍去

1933年3月16日，在喜峰口长城败退下来的日寇，重新组成6000多人的步炮联队，先后在50多架次飞机、多门重炮和数十挺轻重机枪的掩护下，向我马蹄峪、罗文峪、山寨峪、沙坡峪长城隘口发起猛攻，500多发炮弹炸得罗文峪关口和两翼长城砖石横飞，敌台崩塌。面对暴行，遵化人民倾力支援二十九军奋勇杀敌，白天将士们据关杀敌，夜晚出动300多人大刀队摸进敌营，斩杀倭寇。三天的罗文峪恶战，二十九军将士以极其简陋的武器，斩杀日伪军1000多人，关外10里再无寇影，后又在石门击落日机一架。二十九军将士在罗文峪一线长城用生命和鲜血谱就了一曲威震敌胆的《大刀进行曲》。

Beheading Japanese Invaders' with Broadswords

On March 16, 1933, the Japanese invaders retreating from their defeat at the Xifeng Pass formed a joint troop of infantry and artillery, and ferociously attacked the passes of the Great Wall at Mati Valley, Luowen Valley, Shanzhai Valley and Shapo Valley with the support of over 50 times of aircraft attacks, many heavy cannons and several dozens of light and heavy machine guns. Over 500 bombs blasted the bricks and stones of the Luowenyu Pass and the two walls along it, causing the collapse of watchtowers. In face of the atrocity, Zunhua people went all out to support the 29th Army to fight against the enemy. In daytime, soldiers fought the enemy at passes; at night, they dispatched a broadsword team to kill Japanese invaders in their camp. During the three-day fierce battle at Luowen Valley, soldiers of the 29th Army killed over 1,000 soldiers of the Japanese puppet army with simple weapons. No enemy was present within 10 *huali* beyond the Great Wall. Later, a Japanese aircraft was shot down at Shimen. With their lives and blood, the soldiers of the 29th Army composed the song of the *Broadsword March* that struck terrors into the enemy's hearts along the Great Wall near Luowen Valley.

上图：
罗文峪长城上严阵以待的
二十九军将士
Picture above:
The 29th Army soldiers in battle
array on the Great Wall at Luowen Valley

下图：
二十九军阵亡战士墓
Picture below:
Tomb of the soldiers
of the 29th Army killed in battle

罗文峪长城抗战掩体
Shelters for operations against
Japanese aggression on the Great Wall
at Luowen Valley

依托长城反扫荡

继第一、二、三次日寇强化治安后，1942年4至9月，日寇调集其精锐部队二十七师团的4个联队和伪军计9万余人，采取"梳篦清剿，辗转剔抉，逐步吞食"策略，对遵化及周边实施了更为残酷的第四、五次强化治安，以达到将冀东沦为"大东亚战争后方基地"的罪恶目的。遵化北部抗日军民开展了针锋相对的反扫荡斗争。马兰峪、罗文峪、洪山口等长城沿线村和关口，建立秘密联络站和抗日物资供应基地，以长城为依托实行多种形式的坚壁清野，有力保障了反围剿战斗的顺利开展。

Operations on the Great Wall against the Enemy's Mopping-up Campaign

Following their first, second and third strengthening of control, from April to September 1942, the Japanese invaders assembled over 90,000 soldiers of four wings of its elite troops of the 27th Division as well as its puppet army and implemented even crueler fourth and fifth strengthening of control over Zunhua and its surrounding areas based on the strategy of combing out rebels and gradually devouring the territory. In doing so, Japan aimed to reduce the eastern part of Hebei to a rear base for its Great War in East Asia. To fight against the Japanese invasion, both the Chinese army and villagers established secret liaison stations and material supply bases in villages and passes along the Great Wall such as Malan Valley, Luowen Valley and Hongshan Pass. Various forms were used to strengthen the defense and clear the fields backed up by the Great Wall, which greatly guaranteed the smooth proceeding of the campaign against Japanese encirclement and suppression.

洪山口
The Hongshan Pass

洪山口——
冀东第一个抗日游击根据地

1938年冀东抗日武装大暴动西撤失败，冀东民众抗日运动陷入了低谷，包森受命带领28名同志开赴洪山口，以长城做屏障开始了敌占区抗日游击根据地创建活动。他们凝聚抗战力量，扩大抗战武装，发展党的组织，建立地方政权，组织民众反扫荡，端据点，擒匪首，灭日寇，根据地很快由一个关隘和狭长山沟发展到冀东五县，人口30多万，振奋了冀东人民，打击了日寇嚣张气焰，为坚持冀东敌后游击战开创了新局面。

The Hongshan Pass—
the First Anti-Japanese
Guerrilla Base in East Hebei

In 1938, when the Armed Anti-Japanese Rebellion in East Hebei failed in western retreat, the anti-Japanese movement of the people in the region was at a low ebb. Bao Sen was ordered to lead 28 comrades to the Hongshan Pass, starting the establishment of an anti-Japanese guerrilla base in the area occupied by the enemy. They gathered forces against Japanese aggression, expanded armed forces, developed party organizations, established local regime and organized people to resist the enemy's mopping-up campaign. Removing the enemy's strongholds, capturing bandit leaders, and killing Japanese invaders, the soilders rapidly expanded the base from a pass and a narrow valley to five counties in East Hebei, with residents of over 300,000. This encouraged the people in East Hebei, suppressed Japanese invaders' arrogance, and opened up a new situation for promoting in the guerrilla warfare in the enemy's "backyard" in East Hebei.

马蹄峪洼子楼
The tower at the Mati Valley

洼子楼里审池本

1939年4月26日，侵华日军驻遵化宪兵队长、裕仁天皇的表弟、伪康德皇帝妹夫池本信次郎，带一汽车警备队押着被捕的王振锡（包森司令警卫员）去长城一带找包森劝降。王施巧计在北十里铺村甩掉警备队，只把池本、翻译带到了正在张家坟村北伪装脱坯的八路军战士跟前，副大队长年焕兴、班长贾振远和战士们迅速缴了池本的械，把他拖到马蹄峪关洼子楼里审问，听警备队枪声渐进，池本以为救援已到，拒不服审认罪，战士们无奈只好把他拖到岭后，王振锡三板斧砍死池本。日本特务川岛芳子想让八路军提条件赎回池本尸体，包森响当当地说："条件俩：日本投降；滚出中国！"

Bringing Ikemoto to Trial in the Tower at Mati Valley

On April 26, 1939, Ikemoto shinjiro, head of the Military Police Corps of the Japanese army in Zunhua, cousin of Emperor Hirohito, and brother-in-law of Emperor Kangde of the puppet state of Manchukuo, escorted Wang Zhenxi (Commander Bao Sen's guard) who was under arrest with a truck of armed police to the Great Wall, seeking to induce Bao Sen to capitulate. Wang played a trick to get rid of the armed police in the village of Northern Shilipu and only took Ikemoto and an interpreter to the soldiers of the Eighth Route Army, who were disguised as puppet army soldiers at the north of the Zhangjiafen Village. Deputy battalion head Nian Huanxing, squad leader Jia Zhenyuan and other soldiers rapidly disarmed Ikemoto and pulled him to the tower at Mati Valley for trial. Hearing the approaching of the gunshots of his armed police, Ikemoto refused to admit his guilt. The soldiers of the Eighth Route Army had no choice but to pull him to the rear of the ridge, and Wang Zhenxi killed him with an axe. When the Japanese spy Kawashima Yoshiko asked the Eighth Route Army to raise conditions for the return of Ikemoto's body, Bao Sen said firmly, "two conditions: Japan surrenders; Japanese get out of China!"

凤凰岭长城
The Great Wall at Fenghuang Ridge

长城脚下毙山口

凤凰岭饿老婆顶寨是日寇在遵化长城沿线制造的两大"人圈"之一，囚禁无辜百姓2400人。这里有一杀人不眨眼的恶魔山口正雄，麾下有一无恶不作的伪满洲队，东陵和马兰峪人恨极。1941年8月的一天，包森经过缜密侦查和精心部署，率13团一部和遵兴游击队，采取"引蛇出洞"和"诱敌入瓮"战术，在凤凰岭长城脚下击毙山口正雄，全歼参战日伪军，缴获汽车2辆，迫击炮2门，轻机枪4挺，为民除恶报了仇。

Killing Yamaguchi at the Foot of the Great Wall

The Elaopoding Stockaded Village at Fenghuang Ridge was one of the two "human pens" made by Japanese invaders along Zunhua section of the Great Wall, imprisoning 2,400 innocent people. Yamaguchi Maruyama was a demon there, slaughtering without batting an eyelid. The puppet Manchu troop led by him would never hesitate at committing any evils, for which, people in Dongling and Malan Valley hated them intensely. One day in August 1941, after careful investigation and painstaking deployment and adopting the tactics of luring the snakes out of the holes and inducing the enemy into a jar, Bao Sen, led the first troop of the 13th Regiment and Zunxing Guerilla Troop, killed Yamaguchi Maruyama at the foot of the Great Wall at Fenghuang Ridge, exterminated all Japanese and puppet troops in the battle, and captured two vehicles, two mine throwers, and four light machine guns. In doing so, he removed the evils and avenged the sufferings of people there.

千叶命丧古城

始建于洪武年间，后改为蓟镇马兰路路城的马兰峪，1937年被日寇划为伪满特区，日本裕仁天皇的妻侄千叶弥次郎出任特区总务、谍报课长。他以办学为名大肆实施文化侵略，亲手杀害我志士仁人和无辜百姓100多人。1944年5月8日，八路军战士胡凤岐、高连太、张申、高永祥在马兰峪横街"明盛客栈"里击毙了罪大恶极的特务头子千叶。

Chibamijiro Lost His Life in an Ancient Town

Malan Valley, established in the Hongwu reign of the Ming dynasty and later change to Malanlu of Jizhen Garrison, was chosen by Japanese invaders as a special zone for their puppet army in 1937. Chibamijiro, the nephew of Emperor Hirohito's wife, acted as director of the special zone and supervisor of espionage. In the name of running schools, he wantonly conducted cultural aggression, and personally killed over 100 party members and innocent people. On May 8, 1944, 4 soldiers of the Eighth Route Army, i.e. Hu Fengqi, Gao Liantai, Zhang Shen and Gao Yongxiang killed the crime-ridden spy head Chibamijiro at the Mingsheng Hotel on the Hengjie Street of Malan Valley.

古城马兰峪
Ancient town at Malan Valley

被日寇轰炸后的沙坡峪敌台
Shapoyu Watchtower after bombing
by Japanese invaders

不垮的敌台

1942年春，14军分区干部纪润身和沙坡峪党支部负责人纪德存，率众在敌台中掩藏了360匹大布，5000多包桐油，400多斤炸药，20多箱手榴弹和30000斤粮食。当得知有人告密后，立即组织群众将物资转移到附近山洞中，躲过了敌人的搜剿。纪润身、老党员邢德福、13团侦查员王永凭借长城与日寇展开了殊死搏斗，子弹打光了，就用砖头石块砸，并乘机跳下长城脱险。纪润身带伤跑到邦宽大道张家洼段和同志们一起埋地雷，炸毁日寇4辆军车，迫使敌人放弃了对这批军用物资的再次搜剿。

The Unassailable Watchtower

In the spring of 1942, Ji Runshen, a Party member of the 14th Military Sub-area, and Ji Decun, a leader of the Shapoyu Party Branch, led people to store 360 *pi* (unit of measurement; 1 *pi* is equivalent to 33.3m) cloth, over 5,000 bags of tung oil, over 400 *jin* (unit of measurement; 1 *jin* = 0.5kg) explosives, over 20 boxes of grenades, and 30,000 *jin* grains in a watchtower. Learning that the whereabouts of the materials stored there were divulged, they immediately organized people to transfer the materials to a cave nearby, thus sheltering them from the enemy's raid. Ji Runshen, a senior Party member Xing Defu, and an investigator of the 13th Regiment Wang Yong engaged in a life-and-death battle with Japanese invaders. When their bullets were exhausted, they smashed the enemy with bricks and stones. They finally escaped by jumping off the Great Wall. Ji Runshen, despite his wounds, ran to the Zhangjiawa section of the Bangkuan Road to bury landmines together with other comrades, which bombed four military trucks of the Japanese invaders, thus forcing the enemy to give up their second search for these military materials.

火烧禅林寺

坐落在长城脚下的禅林古寺，初曰云昌，始建年代无考，后秦的弘始年间（399-415）重修，唐、辽继修后改曰禅林。抗战时期禅林寺是冀东八路军的主要落脚点和临时指挥所，1939年4月擒拿处决日本宪兵池本大佐后，包森司令员就是在这里用斋饭和寺庙住持、八路军战士举行庆功宴的。当年的"五次强化治安"日寇盗走寺内12座铜佛和所有文物后，一把大火焚烧了华北著名的千年古刹。至今，古老的银杏树上还留有当年树干被烧的炭痕。

The Burning of Chanlin Temple

The ancient Chanlin Temple at the foot of the Great Wall, originally called Yunchang, was first built in the remote unrecorded time, restored in the Hongshi reign of the Later Qin period (399-415), and renamed Chanlin after its reconstruction in the Tang and Liao dynasties. During the period of the War of Resistance against Japanese Aggression, Chanlin Temple was the main foothold and temporary command post of the East Hebei Eighth Route Army. In April 1939, after capturing and killing the Japanese military policeman Ikemoto Taisa, Commander Bao Sen held a victory banquet of vegetarian food with the temple abbot and soldiers of the Eighth Route Army. During the Fifth Strengthening of Control activity, Japanese invaders stole 12 bronze Buddhist statues and all cultural relics in the temple before they burned the 1,000-year-old ancient temple. By far, the char traces on the trunk of an ancient gingko tree still remain.

左图：
被日寇炸毁的禅林寺遗址
Picture on the left:
Ruins of Chanlin Temple bombed by Japanese invaders

右图：
2000年重修后的禅林寺
Picture on the right:
Chanlin Temple restored in 2000

四野进关

1948年11月23日，胜利完成辽沈战役的四野百万大军开始
进关，随行的还有10万匹战马和15万民工。12月1日，大军分
别由三屯营、洪山口、罗文峪陆续挺进遵化。县委、县政府速
发《火急通令》通令全县和各兵站防敌防特，做好供给，确
保大军顺利过遵。遵化人民为欢迎子弟兵的到来，路桥平整，
清水洒街，得胜牌楼遍布路口，迎庆锣鼓震耳欲聋，秧歌声
欢迎声此起彼伏。部队行至邦宽大道，立刻由四路纵队变为
六路纵队，威严雄壮，气势昂扬，战马嘶鸣，口号震天；百
姓夹道迎送，端茶递饭，热泪盈眶。四野进关临时指挥部设
在遵化城西北的张各庄，林彪、罗荣桓、肖劲光、邓子恢等
首长亲自坐镇指挥，大军三天三夜过完后，立即打响了平津
战役。

The Fourth Field Army Entered the Great Wall

On November 23, 1948, the Fourth Field Army of one million
soldiers, which had just triumphed in the Liaoxi-Shenyang
Campaign, started to march towards the Great Wall, followed
by 100,000 war horses and 150,000 migrant workers. On
December 1, the army successively marched into Zunhua from
Santun Garrison, Hongshan Pass and Luowen Valley. The CPC
County Committee and the County Government immediately
issued an *Urgent Circular* to notify that the whole county and
all military stations should be on guard against enemies and
spies and prepare supplies to ensure that the army pass through Zunhua smoothly. Zunhua people leveled the roads,
cleaned the streets, erected triumphant archways everywh-
ere, played gongs and drums, and danced to welcome the
army. The troops, upon arrival at the Bangkuan Road, turned
from four columns to six, dignified and high-spirited, with
neighing horses and earth-shaking shouts. Local people presented them with tea and food and saw them off with tears
in eyes. The temporary command headquarters of the Fourth
Field Army were in Zhangge Village northwest of Zunhua city.
Leaders such as Lin Biao, Luo Ronghuan, Xiao Jinguang and
Deng Zihui led the army personally. As soon as the army passed through Zunhua, which took for three days and three
nights, the Beiping-Tianjin Campaign started.

四野在张各庄的临时指挥部
The temporary command headquarters
of the Fourth Field Army in Zhangge Village

二十世纪七十年代的西下营民兵
Militiamen of Xixia Garrison in the 1970s

二十世纪七十年代
西下营民兵营司号员吴占兴

Wu Zhanxing, a bugler of
Xixiaying Militia in the 1970s

长城军号又响起

1969年珍宝岛之战败为下风的苏联恼羞成怒，决计要对中国实施几百万吨级当量的核打击，毛泽东得报后淡淡一笑，"不就是要打核大战嘛，鄙人不怕！"他大手一挥，"人不犯我，我不犯人。人若犯我，我必犯人！""六亿人民六亿兵，万里江山万里营"，长城上响起了嘹亮的练兵军号。

全国人大确立每年的9月3日为"抗日战争胜利纪念日"后，压抑已久的当年大安口民兵连小司号员张凤登上长城，又吹响了久违的进军号。

Bugles Were Sounded again on the Great Wall

当年的小司号员张凤
Zhang Feng, a little bugler in the past

In 1969, the former Soviet Union, frustrated at its failure in the battle on the Zhenbao Island, decided to launch a nuclear attack equivalent to several million tons of TNT against China. Mao Zedong, upon learning the news, smiled, "It's just a nuclear war. I'm not afraid!" Waving his hand, he said, "We will not attack unless we are attacked; if we are attacked, we will certainly counter-attack!" "600 million people are 600 million soldiers, and a land of 10,000 *li* is a military camp of 10,000 *li*." Troop training bugles were sounded on the Great Wall.

After the National People's Congress of China determined September 3 of each year as the Victory Day of the Chinese War of Resistance against Japanese Aggression, Zhang Feng, a past bugler of the militia at the Da'ankou Pass, ascended the Great Wall to sound a march bugle not heard for long.

长城是咱后院墙

遵化市面积1521平方公里，人口73万，长城横贯其境。在外问起老家，遵化人总是自豪地说："长城是咱后院墙！"是的，长城就在遵化北郊，早起遛弯几步就上了长城。

The Great Wall Serves as Our Backyard Wall

The Great Wall runs through Zunhua city, which covers an area of 1,521km² with a population of 730,000. When they are away from their hometown, Zunhua people would always say proudly, "The Great Wall is our backyard wall!" This is true. The Great Wall is located in the northern suburbs of Zunhua, and one can reach there after several minutes of walk.

后杖子长城
The Great Wall at Houzhangzi Village

遵化因城而立

遵化长城的九门雄关，战时是拒敌的要塞，平时是游牧部落和农耕民族互市交往的通道，因通关而设了买马监，因边战而兴旺了冶铁业，遂在俊糜、徐无、无终的基础上，于后唐（925）始设县治。明时因战略位置不断提升而成为驻有三卫一所三营（遵化卫、忠义中卫、东胜右卫、宽河守御千户所、左营、右营、辎重营）和顺天巡抚的军事重镇，清时成州，民国复县，1992年撤县建市，2006年被联合国教科文组织中国专家组评定为千年古县。

Zunhua City was Established for Its Vicinity to the Great Wall

The nine passes on Zunhua section of the Great Wall are strongholds for resisting the enemy in wartime, and are passages for the exchanges between nomadic tribes and farming nationalities in peaceful time. The horse market was set up for frontier trade, and the metallurgical industry flourished because of border wars. On the basis of Junmi, Xuwu and Wuzhong, a county was established here in the Later Tang dynasty (925). In the Ming dynasty, due to its improving strategic position, it developed into a strategic military garrison consisting of sub-garrisons of three *wei*, one *suo* and three *ying* garrisons (Zunhua Wei, Zhongyi Middle Wei, Dongsheng Right Wei, Kuanhe Thousand Household Bureau of Defense, Left Garrison, Right Garrison, and Zizhong Garrison) and a Shuntian Grand Coordinator. In the Qing dynasty, it was turned into a prefecture. In the period of the Republic of China, it became a county again. In 1992, it was established as a city. In 2006, it was rated by the Chinese expert team of UNESCO as a 1000 -year-old ancient county.

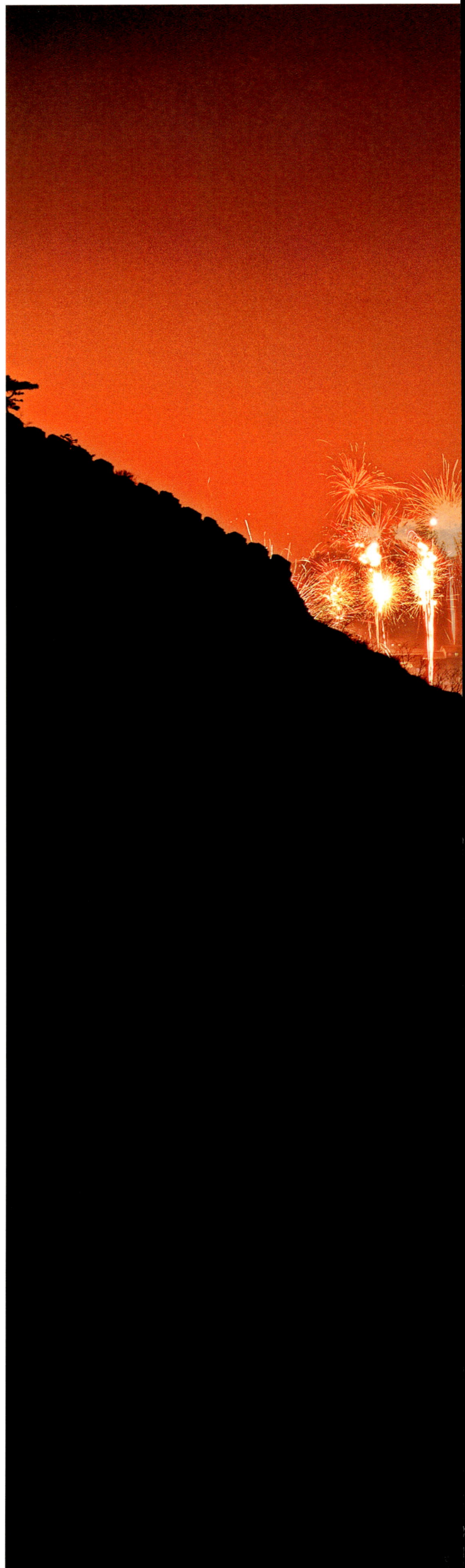

罗文峪长城
The Great Wall at Luowen Valley

遵化因城而名

久经长城雄风熏陶的遵化人民，建国后，以特有的长城精神改河山，建家园，五十年代西铺"穷棒子社"被毛主席誉为整个国家的形象，六十年代沙石峪被周总理誉为活愚公，七十年代五小工业享誉世界，撤县建市后连续九年跻身全国县域经济百强，中国全面小康成长型百佳县（市），建设创新型国家百强县（市），福布斯中国大陆最佳县级城市25强和中国循环经济优秀品牌城市，遵化社会、经济发展驶入了快车道。

人间仙境 — 遵化
A wonderland on earth—Zunhua

Zunhua Becomes Famous for the Great Wall

The people of Zunhua, since the establishment of the People's Republic of China, have been rebuilding their hometown with their unique spirit nurtured by the mightiness of the Great Wall. In the 1950s, the cooperative formed by poor peasants of Xipu was extolled by Chairman Mao as the image of the whole country. In the 1960s, the Shashiyu Village was lauded by Premier Zhou Enlai as the contemporary Foolish Old Man moving the mountain. In the 1970s, five small industrial enterprises (producing iron and steel, coal, chemical fertilizer, cement and machinery) were well known all over the world. After the establishment of Zunhua City, it was listed among China's top 100 counties in terms of economic strength for nine years in a row, top 100 counties (cities) for all-round wellbeing, top 100 innovative counties, Forbes top 25 county-level cities of the Chinese mainland, and an excellent city in circular economy of China. The social and economic development in Zunhua has driven into a fast track.

栗花簇拥的廖家峪长城
The Great Wall at the Liaojia Valley nestling in chestnut flowers

徐达植栗

因土质适宜，京东板栗为遵化以东的长城沿线的最佳经济作物，树最盛，果最佳。朱元璋于洪武十四年（1381）派大将徐达督修长城时，特传旨划山屯田，让戍边军户边修长城，边植栗树，板栗成了当时修城戍边军民的养身之果。燕王朱棣登基后特封他多次栖身过的城子峪北山为"栗山"，山顶为"燕王台"。戚继光镇边16年，年年修长城，岁岁植栗树，边境安宁，边民富足。明清两朝遵化板栗是朝廷贡果，遵化也是享誉世界的"京东板栗之乡"，现在遵化年产优质板栗2万吨，涌现出了"栗源"等一批大型板栗精加工企业。

Xu Da Planted Chestnut Trees

Due to proper soil, chestnut trees are the best cash plant for the area along the Great Wall east of Zunhua, with most luxuriant trees and best fruits. In the 14th year of the Hongwu reign (1381), when dispatching General Xu Da to supervise the building of the Great Wall, Zhu Yuanzhang especially ordered that military households on the border should plant chestnut trees while building the Great Wall. Thus chestnuts became the staple food for soldiers and civilians on the border. After Prince of Yan Zhu Di ascended the throne, he especially conferred the name Mount Chestnut to the northern mountains by the Chengzi Valley where he had stayed for several times and the name Prince of Yan's Platform to the mountain top. During the 16 years when Qi Jiguang governed the border, he built the Great Wall and planted chestnut trees each year, when the border was at peace and people on border led a rich life. During the Ming and Qing dynasties, Zunhua chestnuts were tributary fruits to the court, Zunhua was also the homeland of Jingdong chestnuts celebrated in the world. Now, Zunhua produces 200,000 tons of excellent chestnuts each year, and a number of enterprises for highly processed chestnut food such as Liyuan have emerged.

上图：
石崖岭寨长城栗花
Picture above:
Chestnut flowers on the Great Wall at Shiyaling Stockaded Village

下图：
京东板栗
Picture below:
Jingdong Chestnuts

大百年栗树已成王
A 600-year-old chestnut tree

舍身台长城
The Great Wall at Sheshen Platform

皇妃采枣

正德二年（1507）秋，才女皇妃侍驾武宗朱厚照东巡驻跸遵化汤泉行宫，忽闻兀良哈一万骑兵喜峰口犯边，武宗率三千精兵出关截击，斩获无算，犯敌大败而逃。武宗擒敌，皇妃独自呆在汤泉行宫中好不忧闷，遂在池壁题诗一首：沧海隆冬也异常，小池何事暖如汤？溶溶一脉流今古，不为人间洗冷肠。诗成仍不胜烦，便由宫女陪伴缓步登上汤泉茅山。时值金秋，山坡尽是红灿灿、圆溜溜的酸枣，皇妃悦甚，口哼小曲忘情地摘起了酸枣，满载而归后，御医连说："酸枣，宝贝，宝贝！安五脏，轻身延年，熟用治不眠，生用治好眠。"自此，酸枣竟陪伴皇妃终老一生。

An Imperial Concubine Picked Wild Jujubes

In the autumn of the 2nd year of the Zhengde reign (1507), a talented imperial concubine accompanied Zhu Houzhao, historically known as Emperor Wuzong, in his tour of inspection in the east, and stayed at the Tangquan Palace of Zunhua. At the news that Uriankhai led a cavalry of 10,000 cavalries to invade the border at the Xifeng Pass, Emperor Wuzong led 3,000 elite soldiers to intercept him, with numerous invadors killed and captured and the rest fled. As the emperor was fighting, the concubine was left alone in the palace. She was so gloomy that she inscribed a poem on the wall by a pond, "The vast sea is chilled in the depth of winter,/Why is this little pond so warm as if being heated?/This balmy spring has been spouting through ages,/But still failing to wash away cold-heartedness in the world." Still fretted after her composition of the poem, she slowly ascended Mount Mao by the hot spring with the company of a palace maid. It was autumn and the whole slope was covered with red and round wild jujubes. The concubine was very pleased and devoted herself to picking jujubes and singing. When she returned with many jujubes, the imperial doctor said again and again, "Wild jujubes, nice, nice! It can calm five internal organs, nourish your body and prolong your life. Eating cooked jujubes can cure insomnia and eating raw jujubes can cure drowsiness." From then on, wild jujubes became important fruit for the concubine in the rest of her life.

戚继光和甄庄贡烟

嘉靖四十二年（1563），烟草由菲律宾吕宋岛传入我国福建漳州地区，封闭的明廷在禁止海上通商的同时还明令禁烟。隆庆二年（1568），戚继光北调蓟镇，随来的戚家军从南方带来了烟草、烟籽和吸烟的习惯，巡边太监奏知隆庆皇帝，皇帝诏问戚继光，戚继光奏称："吸食烟草可使熬夜将士提神、解乏，有助边戍。"隆庆皇帝深解戍士苦处，遂解戒烟之令。铁厂军夫调防，烟草、烟籽随之传入，于是，铁厂周边植烟成习。人们吸来品去，只有与铁厂毗邻的甄庄因土壤成分特殊所产叶子烟最好抽，它"灰白，火亮，味浓，劲冲，不刺喉，不呛嗓"，很快名播四方，最后竟成了朝廷贡烟。

甄庄大叶烟
Big leaf tobacco in Zhenzhuang Village

Qi Jiguang and Tributary Tobacco from Zhenzhuang Village

In the 42nd year of the Jiajing reign (1563), tobacco was introduced to Zhangzhou of Fujian, China, from the Luzon Island of the Philippines. The Ming court practicing the close-door policy banned smoking while forbidding maritime trade. In the 2nd year of the Longqing reign (1568), Qi Jiguang was transferred north to Jizhen Garrison, and the army transferred along with him brought tobacco, tobacco seeds and the habit of smoking from the south. A eunuch inspecting the border reported this to Emperor Longqing. In response to the Emperor's inquiry, Qi Jiguang sent a memorial, saying, "Smoking can refresh soldiers who stay up late, which is good for border defense." Emperor Longqing, deeply understanding the hardships of border soldiers, then lifted the ban on smoking. With the transfer of a garrison at the iron plant, tobacco and tobacco seeds were introduced along with it. As a result, people around the iron plant picked up the habit of smoking. They found that the leaf tobacco produced in Zhenzhuang Village next to the iron plant was of the best quality, as it featured a grey white color, strong smell, and robust taste, yet no irritation to the throat. Soon afterwards, the tobacco became so famous all over the country that it was taken as a tribute to the court.

观音浴日
A Goddess Basking in the Sunshine

山口寨长城
The Great Wall at Shankou Stockaded Village

正统颁诏

遵化长城沿线有铁、金、锰、铬等30多种矿产资源，其中铁储量1.6亿吨，金储量140万吨。唐朝中叶朝廷已在娘娘庄乡小厂开办铁厂，明代最大的冶铁厂是永乐年间在遵化建立的，其山场分布在蓟州、遵化、玉田、滦州、迁安等地。明弘治年间（1488—1505）遵化冶铁达到鼎盛，其中，炼铁炉25座，铸造炉50多座，冶铁工人2500多名，每年炼铁常额为20多万斤，最多达30万斤，是明代中后期最大的冶铁生产基地，史称"遵化铁冶"。正统皇帝在登基之初，便下诏工部："军器之铁止取足于遵化收买。"《明史·食货志五》

The Edict of Emperor Zhengtong on Buying Zunhua Iron

Along Zunhua section of the Great Wall there are over 30 types of mineral resources such as iron, gold, manganese and chromium, including 160 million tons of iron reserves and 1.4 million tons of gold reserves. By the mid-Tang dynasty, the court had opened an iron plant at Xiaochang of Niangniangzhuang Township. The largest iron smelter in the Ming dynasty was built in Zunhua in the Yongle reign, with mines distributed in Jizhou, Zunhua, Yutian, Luanzhou and Qian'an, etc. In the Hongzhi reign (1488-1505) of the Ming dynasty, iron smelting culminated in Zunhua, including 25 blooming furnaces, over 50 foundry furnaces, and over 2,500 iron smelting workers, and regularly producing over 200,000 *jin* iron each year, 300,000 *jin* at most. In the middle and late Ming dynasty, Zunhua became known as the largest iron smelting base. Emperor Zhengtong, in the early period of his reign, issued an edict to the Ministry of Industry, saying "Iron used for military weapons should be bought from Zunhua only." (Vol. 5 of *A Record of Food and Commodities* in *The History of Ming*)

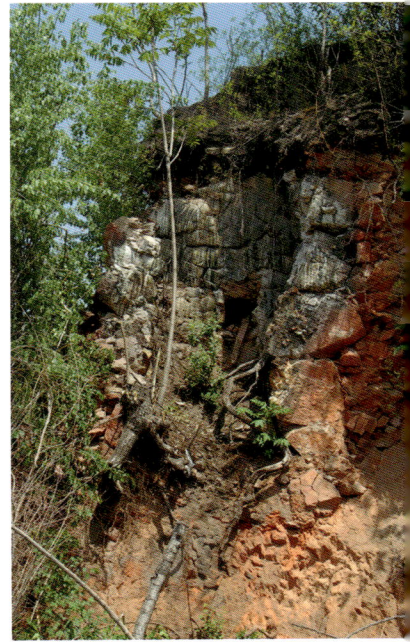

遵化铁厂明冶铁遗址
Ruins of iron smelting of Ming at Zunhua iron plant

依恋长城
Attachment to the Great Wall

唐王锁龙

相传贞观十九年（645），唐王李世民（唐太宗）东征高丽过遵化，发现长城之南、娘娘庄之北有一脉向来自关外的十里大山，气势磅礴，似龙欲飞，唯恐外族成势威胁大唐王朝，除命白袍将军薛礼将长城各关隘增兵布防外，还命其将山南端划一鸿沟以锁龙头，将其中端建一宝塔以镇龙身，并敕名"锁龙山"。今有乡人王洪成率众解其锁，复"卧龙"，置峰建寺，称"腾龙"。如今腾龙寺终日香火不断。

Emperor Taizong of Tang Locked the "Dragon"

It is said that in the 19th year of the Zhenguan reign (645) when Emperor Li Shimin (Taizong of Tang) passed by Zunhua in his east expedition to Goryeo (Korea), he discovered that there was a big mountain range extending ten *li* from outside the border south of the Great Wall and north of the Niangniangzhuang Village, which assumed a great momentum and resembled a dragon about to soar. For fear that a foreign tribe would grow to threaten the Tang dynasty, the emperor ordered White Robe General Xue Li to dispatch more soldiers and strengthen fortifications along the passes of the Great Wall, and had a wide ditch built at the southern end of the mountain to lock the "dragon head", and in the middle of the mountain a pagoda was built to suppress the "dragon body", which was named Mount Suolong (lit. "Locking Dragon"). In the modern age, a native called Wang Hongcheng led a group of people to unlock the mountain, which became a "crouching dragon" again, and built a temple on its peak called Tenglong (lit. "Flying Dragon"). The Flying Dragon Temple receives many pilgrims nowadays.

腾龙寺
The Flying Dragon Temple

朱棣选妃

相传明永乐十九年（1421），前元残余势力鞑靼首领阿鲁台大举犯边，永乐帝朱棣决定再次扫北。为做好战前准备，朱棣亲临遵化的松棚营、白冶庄（铁厂）、磨甲屯（莫家屯）和钉甲岭（丁家岭）视察冶铁铸造和兵器准备情况。朱棣路经一山村，发现一窦氏女子艳绝超群，遂纳入皇宫为妃。窦妃一出，不大的山村很快成了百里闻名的"娘娘庄"。每到麦黄的时节，窦妃娘娘就思念邻村才家相公送她的香白杏，朱棣便命六百里加急到相公庄（相古庄）采摘香白。这个大、皮薄、肉厚、汁甜、味美、离核的大香白杏送进宫来，皇帝爱吃，嫔妃爱吃，宫廷上下都爱吃，相公（古）庄的"满口香"大香白，一时名噪九州，皇封为上上品。

Emperor Zhu Di selected His Concubine

It is said that in the 19th year of the Yongle reign (1421) when Tartar Chief Alutai, a residual force of the former Yuan dynasty, carried out a large military operation to invade the border, Emperor Yongle decided to lead another northern expedition. To make preparations for the war, Zhu Di visited Songpeng garrison, Baye Village (iron plant), Mojia Village and Dingjia Ridge in Zunhua to inspect iron smelting, casting and weapon preparations. When he passed by a village, he discovered an exceptionally beautiful girl of the Dou family and took her as an imperial concubine. The small village soon became famous for having produced an imperial consort. Whenever the harvest season came, Concubine Dou would think of the fragrant white apricots that a man of the Cai's family in a neighboring village had given to her. On knowing this, Zhu Di ordered his men to rush 600 *li* to Xianggong (Xianggu) Village to pick the apricots. The big fragrant white apricot featured thin peel, thick flesh, sweet juice and delicious taste, and was easy to detach from its pit. It soon became a favorite of the emperor and concubines as well as other people in the palace. As a result, it became popular all over the country, and was rated as a top-grade product by the emperor.

遵化长城八大怪

遵化长城不仅以雄奇险峻著称，还以令人叫绝的"八大怪"而驰名。这里的"一步能把千年迈"、"关里有水流关外"、"瓮城在里关在外"、"敌台偎着巨石盖"、"里五外六楼子怪"、"参将修城把佛拜"、"碌碡垒进城墙台"、"钻天缝修城名声坏"，不知迷醉了多少探寻者。

The Eight Wonders on Zunhua Section of the Great Wall

Zunhua section of the Great Wall is famous not only for its magnificence and precipitousness but also for its amazing eight wonders, by which numerous explorers have become fascinated. The eight wonders are Traversing 1,000 years with One Step, Water Inside the Great Wall Flowing Outside, A Barbican Inside the Great Wall, A Watchtower Built on a Huge Rock, A Strange Watchtower with Five Inner Embrasures and Six Outer Embrasures, Officers Building the Wall Worshiped the Buddha, Stone Rollers were Built into a Wall, and Disagreeable Place Names at Zuantianfeng Crack.

平山寨长城
The Great Wall at Pingshan Stockaded Village

一步跨千年！
Take one step to traverse 1,000 years!

一步跨千年的舍身台西
明长城和北齐长城交汇处
The intersection of the Northern
Qi Great Wall and the Ming Great Wall
west of Sheshen Platform where
one can traverse 1,000 years with one step

一步能把千年迈

舍身台寨到马蹄峪关长城因山势陡峭，易守难攻，明长城中断断续续存有大段大段的北齐长城，顺舍身台烽火台西下不远便是北齐长城和明长城交汇处，只一步之差，便是两种边墙，千年时空。逛鹫峰山可别忘了到这儿体验一把"一步越千年"的感受啊！

Traversing 1,000 Years with One Step

The Great Wall extending from Sheshentai Stockaded Village to Mati Valley has large sections of the Northern Qi Great Wall between those of the Ming dynasty because the mountains are precipitous, making it easy to defend and difficult to attack the place. Not far west of the Beacon Tower at Sheshen Platform is the intersection between the Northern Qi Great Wall and the Ming Great Wall. Two kinds of border walls and a thousand years are separated by just one step. This has become a must-visit when one travels to Mount Jiufeng.

关里有水流关外

民谣："长城三千六百口，一万八千楼，只有三关水倒流。"
而遵化就有洪山口、河口两个关口的水，由关里流向关外（另
一关为迁西的喜峰口关）。

Water Inside the Great Wall Flowing Outside

A folk song has it, "Of the 3,600 passes on the Great Wall with 18,000 towers, only three passes see water flow from inside the Great Wall to outside." In Zunhua alone, two passes, namely, Hongshan Pass and Hekou Pass, have water flow from inside the Great Wall to outside (the other being the Xifeng Pass in Qianxi).

由洪山口关流向关外的小河
A little river flowing from Hongshan Pass to outside the Great Wall

由河口关流向关外的小溪
A little stream flowing from Hekou Pass to outside the Great Wall

瓮城在里关在外

罗文峪关是遵化的北大门，战略位置十分冲要。为使关隘坚固，罗文峪关城不仅大城套小城，还在关城东长城里侧山脊上修了一道高于正关的一等边墙，远看就像一个巨大的"♡"，这个"♡"史书说是瓮城。一般瓮城都在城外，可这里的瓮城却修在了关里，这就有点让人匪夷所思了。

A Barbican Inside the Great Wall

The Luowenyu Pass, the northern gate of Zunhua, occupies a critical strategic position. To reinforce the Luowenyu Pass, a layer of big wall were built encircling a smaller one, and a first-grade side wall higher than the regular wall was also built on a ridge inside the Great Wall in the east of the pass. Looking like a huge "♡" from afar, it is a barbican mentioned in historical books. Generally a barbican is built outside the town, but the one here is built inside, which is incredible.

罗文峪关瓮城
The barbican at Luowen Valley

马蹄峪洼子楼
The tower at Mati Valley

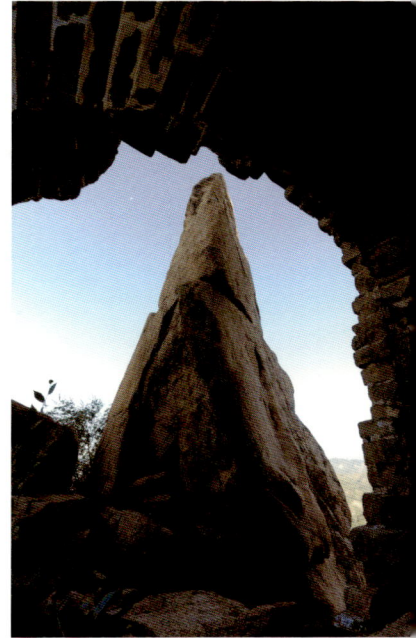

马蹄峪洼子楼
The tower at Mati Valley

敌台偎着巨石盖

据老人讲，长城敌台的修建是十分讲究的，要由风水师根据拒敌需要和山势，反复相度测量才能定址，定址后督修官还要烧香叩拜，祭天祭地。他们把山上巨石怪崖认作是上苍恩赐的吉祥之物，不敢有半点冒犯，这才有了马蹄峪长城巨石、敌台两厢厮守，共同御敌的奇观。面对这尊历经锤打凿琢的长城大修和刀光剑影的战争厮杀竟完好如初，昂然守边的灵性巨石，我们是否也应像崇尚自然的先人那样，对它心存敬畏，呵护有加呢？

A Watchtower Built on a Huge Rock

Old people say that the building of a watchtower on the Great Wall requires meticulousness. A site could be determined only after a geomancer had repeatedly examined the topography and the demands for defending enemies. After the determination of the site, the supervising officer would burn incense and offer sacrifice to Heaven and Earth. They took huge rocks and strange cliffs on the mountains as auspicious signs endowed by Heaven and would not offend them in the least. Thus we have such a wonder on the Great Wall at Mati Valley where a huge rock and a watchtower keep company with each other to jointly resist enemies. In face of this huge rock that remains intact after many overhauls of the Great Wall and fierce battles to bravely guard the border, we'd better hold it in awe and veneration and take care of it just like our ancestors who worshiped nature.

石崖岭寨的"五六眼楼"，
其朝向关内侧墙体上的箭窗数量是五眼。
Watchtower with Five Inner Embrasures and Six Outer Embrasures at Shiyaling Stockaded Village,
with five embrasures on the wall facing inside the Great Wall

里五外六楼子怪

建于洪武年间的石崖岭寨坐落在今兴旺寨乡花椒园子村北，出寨北上，山顶伫立一奇特扁楼。说奇特，是敌台关里关外两侧墙体上的箭窗数量不一致，里侧五眼，外侧六眼，楼内设两券室、三拱道，临时支梯登顶，当地的百姓叫它"五六眼楼"。为啥此楼箭窗里少外多呢？据勘查，楼外山势平缓易攻，也许是多设箭窗便于御敌吧。它是遵化保存最为完好的一所敌台，游遵化长城不可不看此楼。

石崖岭寨的"五六眼楼"，
其朝向关外侧墙体上的箭窗数量是六眼。
Watchtower with Five Inner Embrasures and Six Outer Embrasures at Shiyaling Stockaded Village, with six embrasures on the wall facing outside the Great Wall

A Strange Watchtower with Five Inner Embrasures and Six Outer Embrasures

The Shiyaling Stockaded Village built in the Hongwu reign is located in the north of the present-day Huajiaoyuanzi Village of Xingwangzhai Township. Travelling northward outside the village, we can see a strange flat tower on the top of a mountain. It is strange because the numbers of embrasures in the two walls of the watchtower are not the same, with five inside and six outside. Inside the tower there are two chambers and three archways, with a temporary ladder leading to the top. Local people call it Wuliuyanlou (lit. "Watchtower with Five Inner Embrasures and Six Outer Embrasures"). Why are there more embrasures inside than outside? According to our survey, as the mountains outside the tower are gentle and thus are easy to attack, more embrasures were built perhaps for resisting enemies. This tower is the best preserved one of the kind in Zunhua, and is a must-visit in a tour of Zunhua section of the Great Wall.

参将修城把佛拜

沙岭儿寨有一高2.64米的全国稀有花岗岩石佛，从丰满的造型和遒劲的刀工判断，应为隋唐文物。传万历年间重修长城时事故频发，进展缓慢，十三年（1585）马兰谷参将王通、大安口关指挥佥事周承聘、千总朱松，为求平安，重修了坍圮不堪的石佛寺，并带领修城将士、募夫虔诚地举行了盛大供佛仪式。石佛于1966年被村民偷偷挖坑掩藏，地下沉睡40年后才又重见天日，进寺成佛。登城之余来此上香，庙前万历年间石碑会向你述说石佛帮人修城行善的往事。

沙岭千年石佛
The 1000-year-old
stone Buddha statue on Shaling Ridge

Officers Building the Wall Worshiped the Buddha

In Shaling'er Stockaded Village, there is a 2.64m-high Buddha statue made of granite which was rare in China. Judging from its plump shape and powerful cutting technique, it should be a relic dating from the Sui or Tang dynasty. Legend has it that accidents occurred frequently during the building of the Great Wall in the Wanli reign, leading to slow progress of the work. In the 13th year of the Wanli reign (1585), *canjiang* ((lit. "staff general") officer Wang Tong of the Malan Valley, Commander Zhou Chengpin and brigade commander Zhu Song of the Da'an Pass, rebuilt the destroyed Stone Buddha Temple, and led soldiers and conscripted workers to hold a grand ceremony to make offerings to the Buddha so as to pray for peace and safety. The stone Buddha statue was secretly concealed by villagers who dug a hole to hide it, and was unearthed after 40 years of slumber underground to become the Buddha of the temple again. When you go to the temple to offer incense to the Buddha, a stele of the Wanli reign before the temple will tell you the story of the Buddha helping with the building of the Great Wall.

碌碡垒进城墙台

崇祯二年（1629）年，皇太极十万铁骑犯中原。十月，济尔哈朗率西路军破关涌入大安口直逼遵化，大安口长城遭重创，史称"己巳之变"。崇祯三年（1630）四月，蓟镇总兵杨肇基率部收复了遵化、永平、滦州、迁安四城，八月，紧急修补了大安口、洪山口、龙井关、三屯营等处墙体、敌台、城堡。也许是军情紧急，饥不择食，这次抢修连老百姓的碌碡都垒上了大安口长城。"碌碡打墙"应是"己巳之变"的产物。

Stone Rollers Were Built into a Wall

In the second year of the Chongzhen reign (1629), Huang Taiji invaded the Central Plains leading a cavalry of 100,000 soldiers. In the tenth lunar month, Jirgalang led the Western Column Army to break into the Great Wall through the Da'an Pass, threatening Zunhua. The Great Wall at the Da'an Pass was seriously destroyed. This is called the Jisi Incident in history. In the fourth lunar month of the third year of the Chongzhen reign (1630), Yang Zhaoji, Commander-in-Chief of Jizhen Garrison, recovered Zunhua, Yongping, Luanzhou and Qian'an. In the eigth lunar month, walls, watchtowers and forts at Da'an Pass, the Hongshan Pass, the Longjing Pass and the Santun Garrison were repaired urgently. Perhaps due to the emergency in the military situation, even local peoples' stone rollers were used to repair the Great Wall at the Da'an Pass. This sight is probably a product of the Jisi Incident.

左图：
大安口长城碌碡石
Picture left:
Stone roller on the Great Wall at Da'ankou Pass

右图：
大安口长城碌碡石
Picture right:
Stone roller on the Great Wall at Da'ankou Pass

钻天缝修城名声坏

遵蓟交界处有座海拔895米的凤凰岭，山顶有道3米宽、150米长、40米深的天然裂缝，人称钻天缝，是京东著名风景区。可五百年前这里修长城时，也许是督修官长期野外作业思家恋妇，硬把个秀美山峰叫成了"饿老婆顶"，不远的关寨叫"耻瞎峪"，还有个关口本来绿地宽阔，水肥草美，该叫"宽甸峪"，可硬叫成了长工满沟的"宽佃峪"，还把它们作为关寨名写进了《四镇三关志》。若不是身临其境，只听这仨名真叫你心里添堵呢！

Disagreeable Place Names at Zuantianfeng Crack

At the border between Zunhua and Jizhen, there is Fenghuang Ridge 895m above the sea level, on the peak of which there is a natural crack of 3m wide, 150m long and 40m deep. Known as Zuantianfeng (lit. "Sky Crack"), it is a famous scenic spot east of Beijing. However, when the Great Wall was being built 500 years ago, this beautiful peak was called Elaopo Peak (lit. "Hungry Wife Peak"); a pass not far away, the Chixia Valley (lit. "Shameful and Blind Valley"); and a pass, Kuandian Valley (a valley full of farm laborers) which should have been called the Spacious Fertile Field Valley as it has a stretch of grassland with fertile soil. The reason behind this might be that the supervisor longed for his home and wife in his long-term field work. Also these names have been written into *The Annals on Four Garrisons and Three Passes*. These three names would have discouraged your trip if you had not visited the places personally!

远眺钻天缝
Zuantianfeng Crack viewed from afar

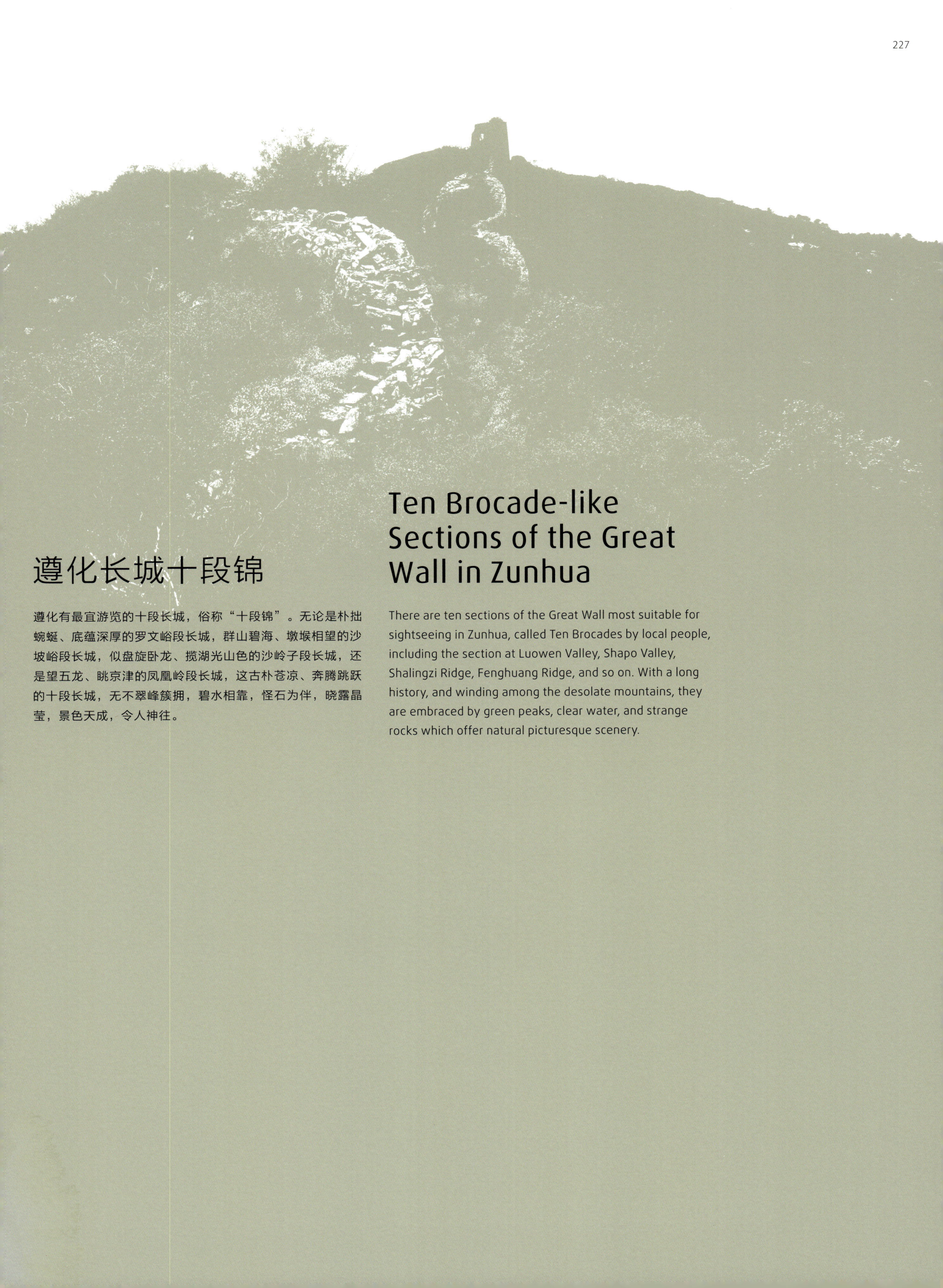

遵化长城十段锦

遵化有最宜游览的十段长城，俗称"十段锦"。无论是朴拙蜿蜒、底蕴深厚的罗文峪段长城，群山碧海、墩堠相望的沙坡峪段长城，似盘旋卧龙、揽湖光山色的沙岭子段长城，还是望五龙、眺京津的凤凰岭段长城，这古朴苍凉、奔腾跳跃的十段长城，无不翠峰簇拥，碧水相靠，怪石为伴，晓露晶莹，景色天成，令人神往。

Ten Brocade-like Sections of the Great Wall in Zunhua

There are ten sections of the Great Wall most suitable for sightseeing in Zunhua, called Ten Brocades by local people, including the section at Luowen Valley, Shapo Valley, Shalingzi Ridge, Fenghuang Ridge, and so on. With a long history, and winding among the desolate mountains, they are embraced by green peaks, clear water, and strange rocks which offer natural picturesque scenery.

长城雄关洪山口
Hongshan Pass

十段锦

Ten Brocade-like Sections of the Great Wall

1

洪山口段长城

The Great Wall at Hongshan Pass

狩猎场上，野鸡峪下。登壮观长城，览古城新貌。

Above the hunting field and below the Yeji Valley. You can ascend the sublime Great Wall to have a view of the new looks of the ancient town.

2

舍身台段长城

The Great Wall at Sheshen Platform

舍身台上，鹫峰岭下。景区北齐长城全国独秀，庙宇高耸，经声悠扬。

Above the Sheshen Platform, and at the foot of Jiufeng Ridge. The Northern Qi Great Wall in the scenic area is unique all over China, with towering temples and melodious sounds of reciting Buddhist sutra.

3

马蹄峪段长城

The Great Wall at Mati Valley

大石峪上，大石峪下。观赏精美敌台，极目遵化古城。

Above and below the Dashi Valley. This is a place to appreciate an exquisite watchtower and look at the ancient city of Zunhua afar.

4

罗文峪段长城

The Great Wall at Luowen Pass

罗文峪关上，甘查峪下。温长城抗战历史，叹长城朴拙蜿蜒。

Above the Luowen Pass and below the Gancha Valley. Here, you can review the history of the War of Resistance against Japanese Aggression on the Great Wall and marvel at its primitive beauty.

5

后杖子段长城

The Great Wall at Houzhangzi Village

后杖子上，山寨峪下。探石、砖长城如何交汇，看遵化最美长城。

Above Houzhangzi Village and below Shanzhai Valley. You can explore how a stone wall is converged with a brick one, and enjoy the most beautiful section of the Great Wall in Zunhua.

6

沙坡峪段长城

The Great Wall at Shapo Valley

付家沟上，刺儿沟下。赏群山碧海，看墩侯相望。

Above the Fujia Trench and below the Ci'er Trench. You can appreciate several forts and beacon towers encircled by lush mountains.

7

冷嘴头段长城

The Great Wall at Lengzuitou Pass

冷嘴头关上，东马道南沟下。山峦低缓，敌台完好，结构怪异。

Above Lengzuitou Pass and below Dongmadao Southern Trench. The mountain range is low and even here,
where there is an intact watchtower with a strange structure.

8

沙岭子段长城

The Great Wall at Shalingzi Valley

鲇鱼池东沟上，沙岭子西沟下。足踏盘旋卧龙，眼眺湖光山色。

Above the eastern trench of Nianyu Pond and below the western trench of Shalingzi. Setting feet on a winding dragon-like wall, you can enjoy the picturesque landscape.

9

鲇鱼石段长城

The Great Wall at Nianyushi Pass

鲇鱼石东沟上，上关湖下。眺鲇鱼守关，看蛟龙入水。

Above the eastern trench of Nianyushi Pass and below Shangguan Lake.
You can enjoy the view of a catfish guarding the pass and watch a dragon-like wall extending into water.

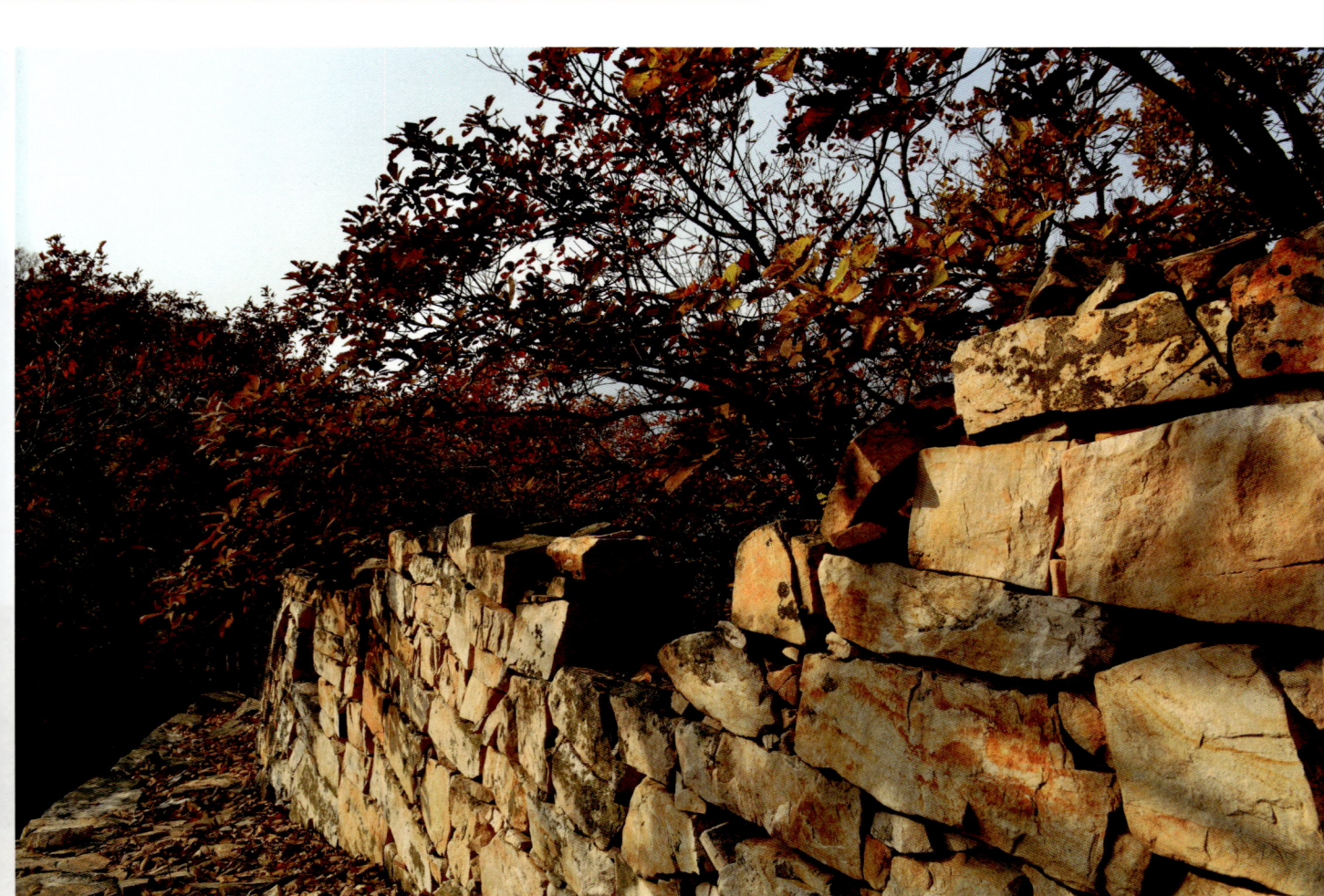

10

凤凰岭段长城
The Great Wall at Fenghuang Ridge

凤凰岭上，钻天缝下。遵化海拔最高，登长城，望五龙，眺京津。
Above Fenghuang Ridge and below Zuantianfeng Crack. It is the highest section of the Great Wall in Zunhua, where you can watch surrounding mountains and gaze at the direction of Beijing and Tianjin.

万里长城永不倒

万里长城历经两千多年的马踏虏平，枪打炮轰，雨浸风蚀，震毁雷击，拆损刻划，已经伤痕累累，弱不禁风，长此以往，"万里长城永不倒"也许就成了远去的童谣。我们应该珍爱，应该养护，应该像呵护自己的生命那样，呵护我们全人类共有的文化瑰宝，让中华民族赖以自豪的万里长城永不倒！

The Great Wall Never Falls

The Great Wall has become wounded all over and might be too weak to pass the test of time after over 2000 years of wars, natural weathering, and other human damage. That the Great Wall never falls in the song might become a remote dream. We should cherish and preserve the common cultural gem of all mankind the way we protect our own life, so that the Great Wall of which the Chinese nation is proud will never fall.

遵化仅剩十八楼

据志书记载，遵化境内共有空心敌台246座，经过四百多年的自然破坏、战争践踏和人为拆毁，目前，较完整的敌台仅剩18座，其中洪山口段6座，马蹄峪段6座，罗文峪段4座，沙坡峪段1座，冷嘴头段1座。大安口以西长城破坏尤为严重，除平山顶峰有座残台外，已无一段完整墙体和可视敌台。这十八座敌台由东向西依次为：廖家峪敌台，洪山口北楼，西安峪敌台，西安峪敌台，白枣峪敌台，河口敌台，天胜寨敌台，天胜寨敌台，舍身台敌台，舍身台敌台，马蹄峪敌台，马蹄峪敌台，甘查峪敌台，甘查峪敌台，前杖子敌台，前杖子敌台，沙坡峪敌台，石崖岭敌台。

Only 18 Watchtowers Are Left in Zunhua

According to historical books, there were 246 hollow watchtowers in Zunhua. After over 400 years of natural destruction, wars, and man-made damage, only 18 watchtowers remain relatively undamaged, including six at Hongshankou Section, six at Matiyu Section, four at Luowenyu Section, one at Shapoyu Section, and one at Lengzuitou Section. In particular, the Great Wall west of Da'ankou Pass was seriously damaged. Except for a residual watchtower on Pingshan Peak, there is no complete wall or visible watchtower. From the east to the west, the 18 watchtowers are respectively: the one at Liaojia Valley, Northern Tower at Hongshan Pass, two at Xi'an Valley, the one at Baizao Valley, the one at Hekou Valley, two at Tiansheng Stockaded Village, two at Sheshen Platform, two at Mati Valley, two at Gancha Valley, two at Qianzhangzi Village, the one at Shapo Valley, and the one at Shiya Ridge.

石崖岭寨长城
The Great Wall at Shiyaling Stockaded Valley

罗文峪"全家福"

Group Photo of Villagers in Luowen Valley

罗文峪全家福

隋代设关、唐代建村的罗文峪，村民多为历代修关筑城和戍边屯田人后裔。饱受边患折磨、战火摧残和日寇蹂躏，他们不屈不挠，劫而复生，人丁兴旺，昂扬向上。1933年3月16日这里爆发了震惊中外的长城抗战，每到这天罗文峪人都要以各种形式祭奠逝去的英烈，追忆大刀击溃日寇的英勇壮举。在长城抗战80周年（1933—2013）到来之际，他们又在击退日寇的敌台下照了一张"全家福"。

Group Photo of Villagers in Luowen Valley

A pass was set up in the Sui dynasty and a village was built in the Tang dynasty in the Luowen Valley. The villagers of Luowen Valley are mostly descendants of builders of the Great Wall and soldiers garrisoning the border and reclaiming wasteland. Having suffered from border invasions, wars and the aggression of Japanese invaders, they have been persevering and enterprising, surviving calamities with a flourishing population. On March 16, 1933, the Battle against Japanese Aggression at the Great Wall took place here. On this day each year, villagers of Luowen Valley will hold a memorial ceremony for martyrs in various forms, in remembrance of their heroic deeds in defeating Japanese invaders with broad swords. On the 80th anniversary of the Battle on the Great Wall (1933-2013), the villagers took a group photo under the watchtower where Japanese invaders were defeated.

后记——
咱给老妈编长城

老妈是个"影膏药"，每逢挂锄时节，她总要跑到咱姥家看几场皮影，回来便没完没了地给我们拉古记。家靠边墙，老妈三句话不离长城，什么"孟姜女哭长城"呀，"罗文守关"呀，"戚继光边墙外揍鞑子"呀……记得小学毕业那年，我忽然天真地对老妈说："妈，等我把字攒多了，就给你编本长城的书！"

半个世纪过去了，老妈早已仙逝。为兑现对老妈的承诺，2011年大年初二，我绷上护膝，装好药片，背上家什，拄着棍子，踏着小雪爬上了沙坡峪西山。还未见长城的影儿，就脚下一滑，一个趔趄摔在了岩石上，得亏棉袄厚，要不，这老腰算是交代了。爬起来，望着倒海而来的群山，一个冷颤打退我好几步，心血管窄，膝关节疼，六十大几的人还爬得了长城？不敢再想，一合眼，老妈的笤帚疙瘩下来了："害怕了？那就别吹着要给我编长城！""不，我不怕！"有老妈督着，一咬牙，我登上了漫无边际的长城……

爬长城是个累活儿，我和侄子俩时常早起四点钟上山，晚上八九点钟还在山上钻荆条棵子。五个烧饼，十一瓶矿泉水，爷俩儿一撑就是十五六个钟头。夏天，褂子湿了干，干了湿，白毛汗出了一身又一身，晚上我软瘫着挪进屋，不等吃饭，人早倒在沙发上过了枕头岭。老伴儿心疼，买来黄瓜西红柿要我带，我不应，为减负只拿矿泉水。老伴儿拗不过，气得"啪啪"把黄瓜西红柿摔一地。我也火了，戳着棍子吼："咱妈从小就没这么娇惯过我！"

麦黄时节，看见长城上有块刻着"忠"字的铭文石，我纳闷儿，"这忠，忠……"念着念着，就蜷在城墙根儿下睡着了。刚合眼，老妈的笤帚疙瘩又来了，"连字都认不透，你拿啥给我编长城？念书去！"老妈这一笤帚疙瘩，把我打进了故纸堆，学明史，读长城，床头、电脑桌全塞满了书。有时为了记住一些年号，弄懂一个事件，半夜三更还皱着眉头在屋里转磨磨儿。朦胧中老伴儿直叹气："我看长城要让你魔怔了！"

2015年11月23日，一尺厚鹅毛大雪，把长城捂得像个大面包。"哇塞，画册正缺山舞银蛇的片子呢！"我们爷儿俩冒险爬上高耸的沙岭长城。从山顶下爬时，一段二十米长、三十度坡的城墙愁住了我们，看着这段没攀没抓的三丈多高城墙，俩腿直发颤。我坐下来慢慢往前蹭，谁知没蹭两步，惯性就推着我飞快向下冲去，冻僵的双手使劲想抓什么，可什么都没得抓，眼瞅俩腿耷拉到墙外，我却戛然停住了。听天由命的我，一合眼，老妈又来了，她托着我的腿："多大了，还这么冒失！不想给妈编长城了？"好一会，侄子爬过来攥住袄领子使劲儿一拎，我才捡了条命。

现如今霾天多，好天少。2013年8月19日又是个响晴天，尽管连续橙色高温预警，可我还是一连四天都在长城上。爬到野鸡峪长城时，毒辣辣的日头把长城烤得处处烫人。突然，一阵虚汗，接着就是眩晕，眼发黑，直想吐，"呀，我的心脏，我的心脏！"捂着胸口，我发疯地冲进前面的残楼，一头倒在瓦砾上。冥冥中老妈把我搂在怀里，亲我的脸说："四头，你瘦了，听妈话，歇两天再爬啊！"我使劲把头扎进妈的怀里，呜呜地哭了，"妈，我想早点儿给你编本长城的书……"

2017年8月11日 于遵化

Postscript – For my Mom, a Book About the Great Wall

My mom was a theater addict. During the off-farming season, she always went to my grandparents' to watch several shadow puppet shows. As soon as she returned home, she showered us with the stories, repeatedly. We lived by the Great Wall, to which my mom constantly alluded to; she couldn't stop making reference to such stories as Lady Mengjiang Crying at the Great Wall, Luo Wen Defending the Pass, Qi Jiguang Defeated the Tatars at the Border Wall, among others. The year when I graduated from primary school, I naively told my mother: "Mom, when I develop a wide vocabulary, I'll make a book about the Great Wall for you!"

It has been more than 50 years since then and my mother had passed away. To fulfill my promise to my mom, on the second day of the Chinese New Year in 2011, I furnished myself with knee pads, a first-aid kit, a backpack of miscellaneous stuff, and a walking stick, and set out up to the West Mountain at Shapo Valley in light snow. Before having any glimpse of the Great Wall, I slipped and tumbled down onto a big bed of rock. Luckily, I wore a thick cotton padded jacket. Otherwise, I got to trade in my old bones. When I got back on my feet, the imposing mountains looked so threatening that sent shivers down my spine. I could not but questioning myself: with a heart problem and failing knees, was I still qualified to hike up to the Great Wall at the age of sixty something? I dared not entertain this thought any further, and with my eyes closed, I heard my mom's lecture whisking down: "Scared now? Then don't brag any more about making a Great Wall book for me!" "No, I'm not frightened!" With this impetus, I toughened up and climbed up the immense Great Wall...

Climbing the Great Wall is a hard work. My nephew and I often get up early and reach the mountaintop at four o'clock in the mornings; we are still forging our way through thorny vines and stalks in the mountains after eight or nine o'clock in the evenings. Only five sesame cakes and eleven bottles of mineral water are enough to sustain the two of us for 15 or 16 hours. In the summer, our shirts are in a wet-dry cycle from sweating. Our entire bodies are just streaming with sweat. At night, I limp back home and pass out on sofa before dinner. This distresses my wife, who makes special effort to buy me cucumbers and tomatoes to bring along. I don't cooperate, holding onto mineral water only for a lighter backpack. Defeated by my stubbornness, my wife gets so mad that she smashes all the tomatoes and cucumbers violently onto the ground. I fire back with shouting: "My mom never spoiled me like this before!"

In one golden autumn, I saw a stone on the Great Wall inscribed with the Chinese character "Zhong (loyalty)," which puzzled me. As I pondered on it, I fell asleep at the foot of the wall. Just then came my mom's whisking lecture, "If there is a character you can't read, what are you going to make me a book of Great Wall with? Go study!" Thus I was swept into piles of historical documents; books on the history of the Ming dynasty and the Great Wall, cluttered the top of my bed and computer desk. Sometimes, I would idle around the room in the depth of the night just to memorize the names of some emperors or to understand a historical event. In the dim light, my wife lamented: "In my opinion, you are mesmerized by the Great Wall!"

On November 23, 2015, a blanket of 1-*chi*-deep (Chinese unit of measurement; 1 *chi* is equivalent to about 33.3cm) snow turned the Great Wall into a big fat loaf of bread. "Wow, our collection is just shy of pictures of a silver dragon dancing in the mountains." So, my nephew and I ventured up to the Great Wall at Shaling Peak. On our way down from the top of the mountain, a section of wall worried us. This section, a 20m-long and 9m-high wall with a gradient of 30 degrees, provided no grip nor grab at all but a terrifying sight. I started out with slowly sliding on my butts; in just two moves, I was lost to the gravity that dragged me down at a flying speed. I desperately tried to grab something with my frozen hands, but there was just nothing to hold on to. All I did was staring ahead until my two legs hanging over the wall and then came a sudden stop. Resigning myself to fate, I shut my eyes. And, there came my mom again, supporting me from under my legs: "How old are you now? Still so reckless! Abandoning the idea to compile a book about the Great Wall for mom?" After a while, when my nephew climbed over and grabbed me by my coat collar, my life was spared.

In recent years, with severe air pollution, we seldom had good weathers. On August 19, 2013, it was another bright sunny day. Despite the continuous excessive heat warning, I was on the Great Wall for four consecutive days. When I reached the Great Wall at Yeji Valley, every inch of the Great Wall was scorching hot. Suddenly, I suffered a burst of cold sweating, followed by dizziness, blackout, and nausea. "Gosh, my heart, my heart!" Clutching at my chest, I dashed frantically into the ruined beacon tower right in front and fell onto the rubble. In an unconscious state, I was cradled by my mom. She kissed my face and said, "Sitou, you got skinnier. Please take my words; rest for several days and then continue!" I buried my head in my mother's arms and cried, "Mom, I just want to produce a book about the Great Wall for you as soon as possible...."

Gao Jingsheng
Zunhua
Aug 11, 2017

创作团队
The Creative Team

❶ 人生原是僧行脚——高景生
Life is originally a monk's traveling
—Gao Jingsheng

❷ 画册里浸满了老伴儿的心血
——李桂芝
The album is saturated with
my wife's painstaking efforts
—Li Guizhi

❸ 砥砺同行，甘苦与共——刘艳利
Share joys and sorrows to
make joint progress
—Liu Yanli

❹ 除了摄影，负重探险他都扛了
——张国华
Besides photography,
he also carries heavy loads
—Zhang Guohua

❺ 攀崖越岭像影子不离我左右
——高良
He is always by my side like a
shadow in climbing cliffs and ridges
—Gao Liang

❻ 除一起爬山外，还要收集长城文物
——安荣斋
Besides climbing mountains
together with us, he has to collect
cultural relics on the Great Wall
—An Rongzhai

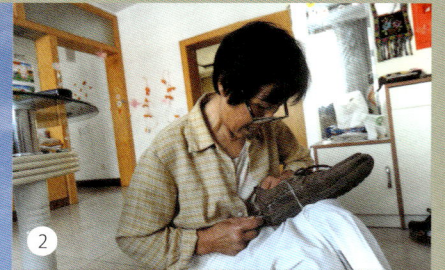

长城不会忘记他们
They won't be forgotten by the Great Wall

图书在版编目（ＣＩＰ）数据

走近长城 —— 遵化长城通览 / 高景生著. –– 北京：
中华书局, 2018.1
ISBN 978-7-101-12989-2
Ⅰ.①走… Ⅱ.①高… Ⅲ.①长城－介绍－遵化 Ⅳ.①K928.77

中国版本图书馆CIP数据核字(2017)第297508号

走近长城 —— 遵化长城通览

策　　　划：韩保平
著　　　者：高景生
封面题签：沈　鹏
责任编辑：许旭虹
摄　　　影：高景生　刘艳利　张国华
艺术指导：朱敬国
装帧设计：北京中绎品牌设计有限公司
译　　　者：陈晓霜　陈兆娟　王巍　王一影
出版发行：中华书局
　　　　　（北京市丰台区太平桥西里38号　100073）
　　　　　http:// www.zhbc.com.cn
　　　　　E-mail: zhbc@zhbc.com.cn
印　　　刷：北京图文天地制版印刷有限公司
版　　　次：2018年1月北京第1版
　　　　　2018年1月第1次印刷
规　　　格：开本787×1092毫米　1/8　印张38
国际书号：ISBN 978-7-101-12989-2
定　　　价：680.00元